The PROGRESSIVE APPROACH to WRITING

Kinder 2

(2ND EDITION)

HAZEL DOMINGO BABIANO
Author

Complete with: teacher's guide, songs and games, and suggested activities for the different learning areas (THEMATIC)

The Progressive Approach to Writing Kinder 2 (2nd Edition)

ISBN: 978-971-625-407-5

First RVC Building, 92 Anonas Cor. K-6th Streets,
East Kamias, Quezon City
Tel. Nos: (02) 8426-5611 | (02) 8573-2380
Telefax No.: 8426-1274
Email: inquiry@stmatthews.ph
Website: www.stmatthews.ph

Note: This book was prepared with the utmost care and scrutiny. Errors which may be discovered while reading the book will be corrected in the next printing. The publisher guarantees the replacement of books received and found to have physical defects like binding and printing, provided that the defects are found before use. Just call telephone nos. (02) 8426-1274 or (02) 8426-5611. The books will be replaced immediately.

Published by **St. Matthew's Publishing Corporation**

PREFACE

A common joke we all make if someone's handwriting is illegible is that perhaps they should become a doctor. Even though the case can be made that handwriting is becoming obsolete since we mostly use cellular phones to communicate and the computer to type everything, handwriting will always be one of the basic tools in the learning toolkit.

Early in the education process, writing the letters of the alphabet often corresponds to learning the letter names and sounds. These skills can be linked to early reading and spelling achievement in that linking the sound (auditory), shape (visual), and formation (kinesthetic) of each letter can build multiple pathways of knowledge into the brain. In addition, children devoting a great deal of time and energy laboring over each letter are tying up their higher level thinking skills used for more advanced mental processes, such as attention to detail of content, organization, evaluation, and synthesis of ideas.

Most people, however, never consider the complexity and difficulty of the writing process. In fact, relative to all other academic activities, writing requires more basic skills than perhaps any other. Writing is a complex act that requires both motor mechanisms and proper effort from the intellect. It is a skill that needs time and enough practice to perfect.

Even during their earliest handwriting exercises, children must combine complex physical and cognitive processes to render letters precisely and fluidly. As writing tasks become more difficult, students must call on an increasingly wide range of skills to correctly form letters, write with enough spacing, and write legibly.

It is primarily with these in mind that this book was designed. This book aims to develop the necessary psycho-physiological mechanisms needed for the mastery of writing, providing logically-arranged activities like preparing to write, where physical skills are practiced, and actual writing, where mental skills are mastered. The activities and exercises in motor and cognitive mechanisms focus not only on learning the step-by-step strokes but also on dexterity and the development of hand and finger muscles to facilitate the proper grip of a pencil. The book offers a variety of activities such as lacing; tearing; cutting; filling in geometric figures with lines; tracing; touching sandpaper alphabets; scribbling; writing the uppercase and the lowercase letters of the alphabet; writing the numerals 1 to 10 and their number words; copying words, phrases, titles, sentences, paragraphs, and homework; writing in script, and writing one's own name. It also seeks to develop in the child an attitude towards writing as a meaningful and fulfilling experience.

In order for the goals of this book to be fully achieved, the teacher is strongly encouraged to give his or her close supervision and guidance to the pupils as they use this book. The teacher must prepare materials such as mats, crayons, scissors, paper, paste, writing insets, and sandpaper alphabets. Believe me, this extra effort will go a long way towards making a **PROGRESSIVE APPROACH TO WRITING!**

Teacher Hazel Domingo Babiano

TABLE OF CONTENTS

I. First Quarter 1-77
- Indirect Preparation for Writing 2
  - Coloring Activity 3
  - Painting Activity 4
  - Lacing Activity 5
  - Tearing Activity 7
  - Cutting Activity 13
  - Clipping Activity 23
- The Basic Writing Strokes 29
- The Writing Insets 41
- The Letters of the Alphabet 45
- Progress Chart 77

II. Second Quarter 78-118
- The Numerals and Number Words 79
- Copying Names and Words
  - Animals 103
  - Colors 107
  - Family Members 109
  - Days of the Week 111
  - Months of the Year 112
  - Action Words 114
  - Describing Words 116
- Progress Chart 118

III. Third Quarter 119-165
- Copying Other Names and Words
  - Things Used and Seen at Home 120
  - Rooms and Spaces in the House 125
  - Things Used and Seen in School 129
  - Places in School 133
  - School Helpers 136
  - Places in the Community 139
  - Community Helpers 144
- Copying Names of Places 147
- Copying Names of People 151
- Copying Phrases 154
- Copying Titles 158
- Copying Sentences 159
- Copying Paragraphs 162
- Copying Homework 164
- Progress Chart 165

IV. Fourth Quarter 166-211
- Preparing to Write in Cursive (Basic Writing Movements) 167
- The Lowercase Letters of the Alphabet
  - The Vowels 178
  - The Consonants
    - Short Letters 180
    - Tall Letters 183
    - Tail Letters 185
- The Uppercase Letters of the Alphabet
  - The Vowels 188
  - The Consonants 190
- Joining Letters 197
- Writing Name in Cursive 202
- Copying Words 203
- Copying Phrases 207
- Copying Sentences 209
- Progress Chart 211

FIRST QUARTER

Teacher's Objectives and Student Evaluation

Lesson	*At the end of the activities, the child should be able to:*			
1	1. refine motor skills through various activities like lacing, tearing, crumpling, cutting, pasting, coloring, painting, and clipping			
	2. hold scissors and pencil correctly			
	3. master the different colors			
	4. make original designs and appreciate art			
2	5. use directionality (left-right, top-bottom, and up-down)			
	6. trace figures and draw straight, slant, and curved lines			
	7. master the different shapes			
3	8. fill shapes with even and regular lines			
	9. refine pencil control while having fun writing			
4	10. master writing the uppercase and lowercase letters of the alphabet on lined paper			
	11. demonstrate uniformity when writing letters			
	12. use uniform spacing between letters			

Legend:  - fairly well  - well 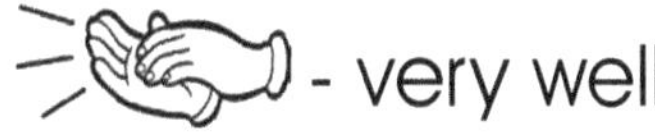 - very well

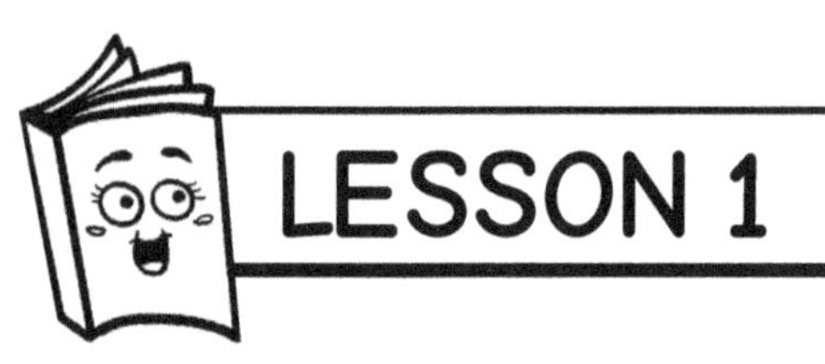

LESSON 1 INDIRECT PREPARATION TO WRITING

Guide: Develop the children's pre-writing skills through various activities like lacing, tearing, crumpling, cutting, pasting, and coloring. These activities are important before children gain basic pencil-control skills. These also lead to the ability to form letters and numbers later on. Progress from short vertical and horizontal lines to more challenging lines such as curves, zigzags, and diagonals.

These are some exercises that will help you refine pencil control and eventually make you write better.

COLORING

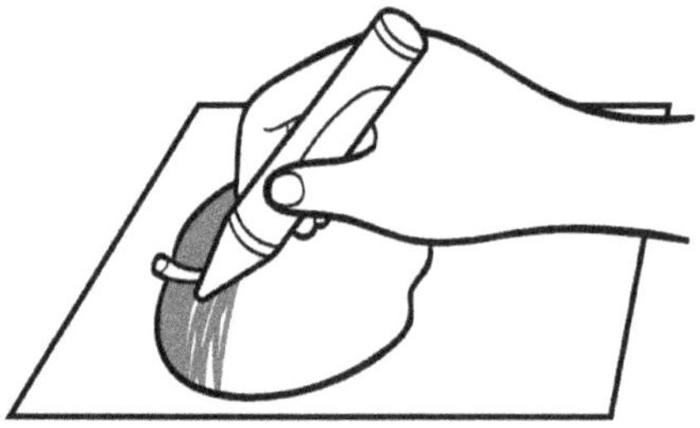

LACING

PAINTING

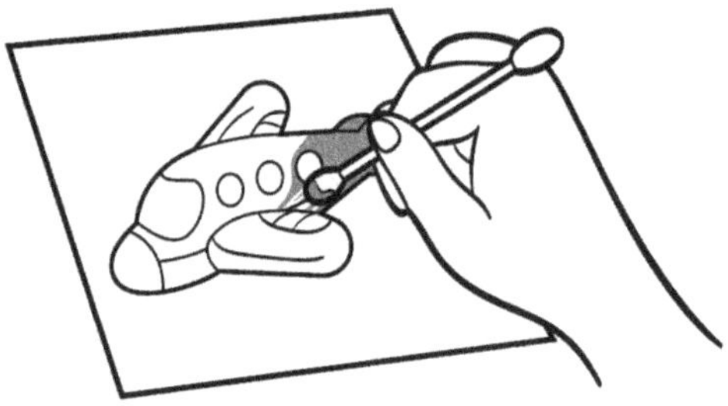

TEARING

CLIPPING

CUTTING

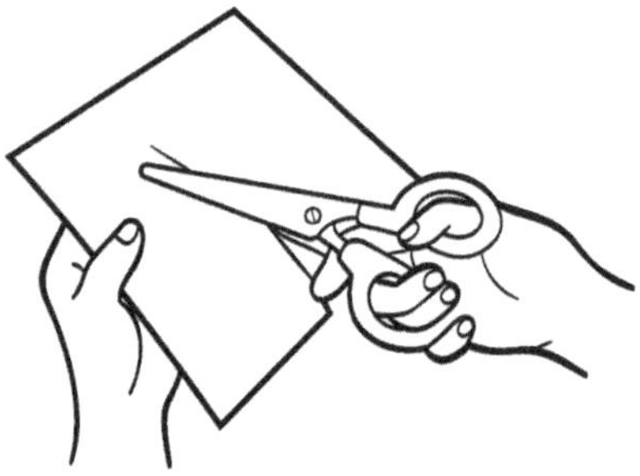

Coloring Activity

ACTIVITY 1

Guide: Have fun reviewing colors and shapes with the children. Let them color the picture below using different colors. Have the children explore and enjoy coloring with their crayons. Have them identify shapes the fun way.

Extended Activity: *Have the children enjoy coloring pages of a workbook, worksheet, and others.*

I got a/an    **today!**

(To the teacher: Encircle the hand gesture that best describes how the child worked on this activity.)

 - fairly well  - well  - very well

____

Teacher's Signature

Painting Activity

ACTIVITY 2

Guide: Practice the children's pincer grip by having them paint the shapes with cotton buds. Review colors and shapes as they paint. Have them follow the color guide below each shape.

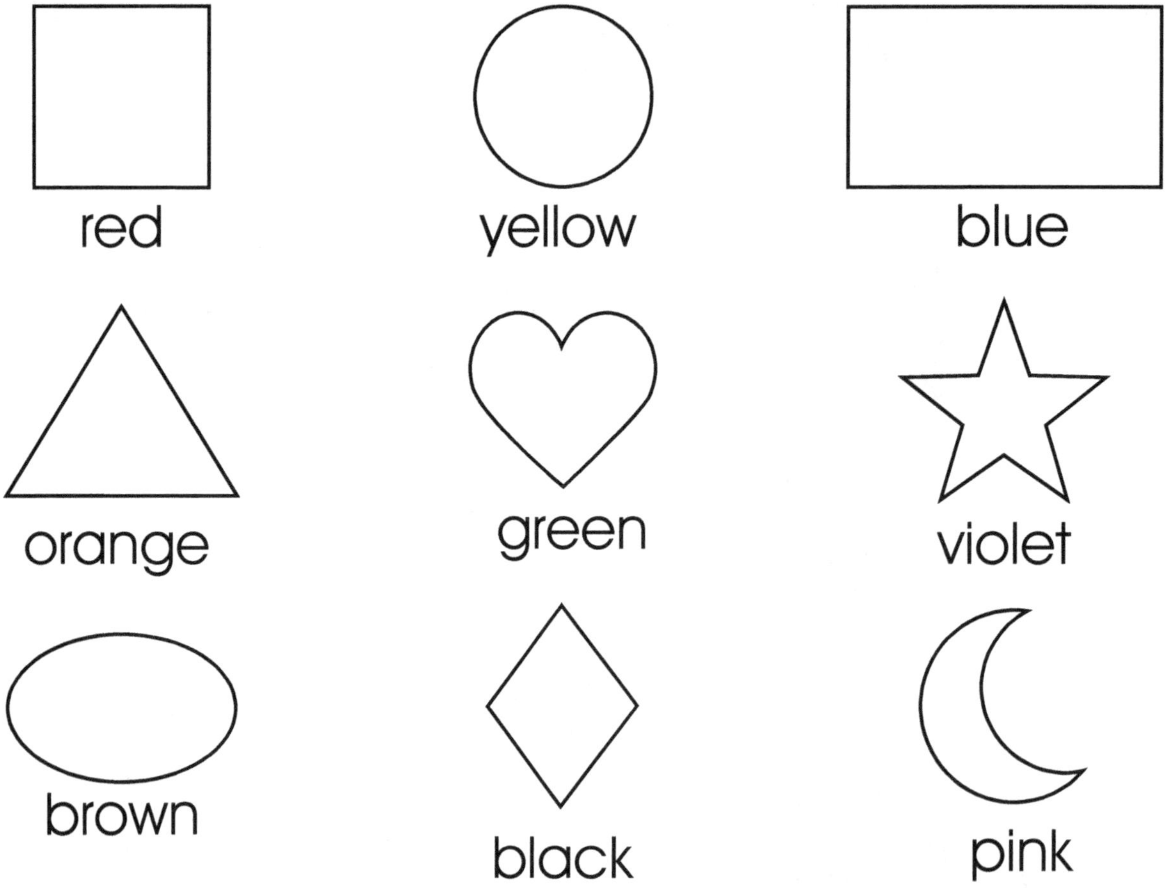

red	yellow	blue
orange	green	violet
brown	black	pink

Extended Activity: *Have the children paint using different materials like cotton, vegetables (vegetable printing), paint brushes, rollers, or even kitchen implements.*

I got a/an    **today!**

(To the teacher: Encircle the hand gesture that best describes how the child worked on this activity.)

 - fairly well  - well  - very well

____
Teacher's Signature

Lacing Activity

ACTIVITY 3

Guide: Have the children paste their family picture onto the frame. Cut along the broken lines. Let the children paste the picture frame onto a cardboard. Punch holes on the dots. Let the children practice lacing up the holes using a shoelace.

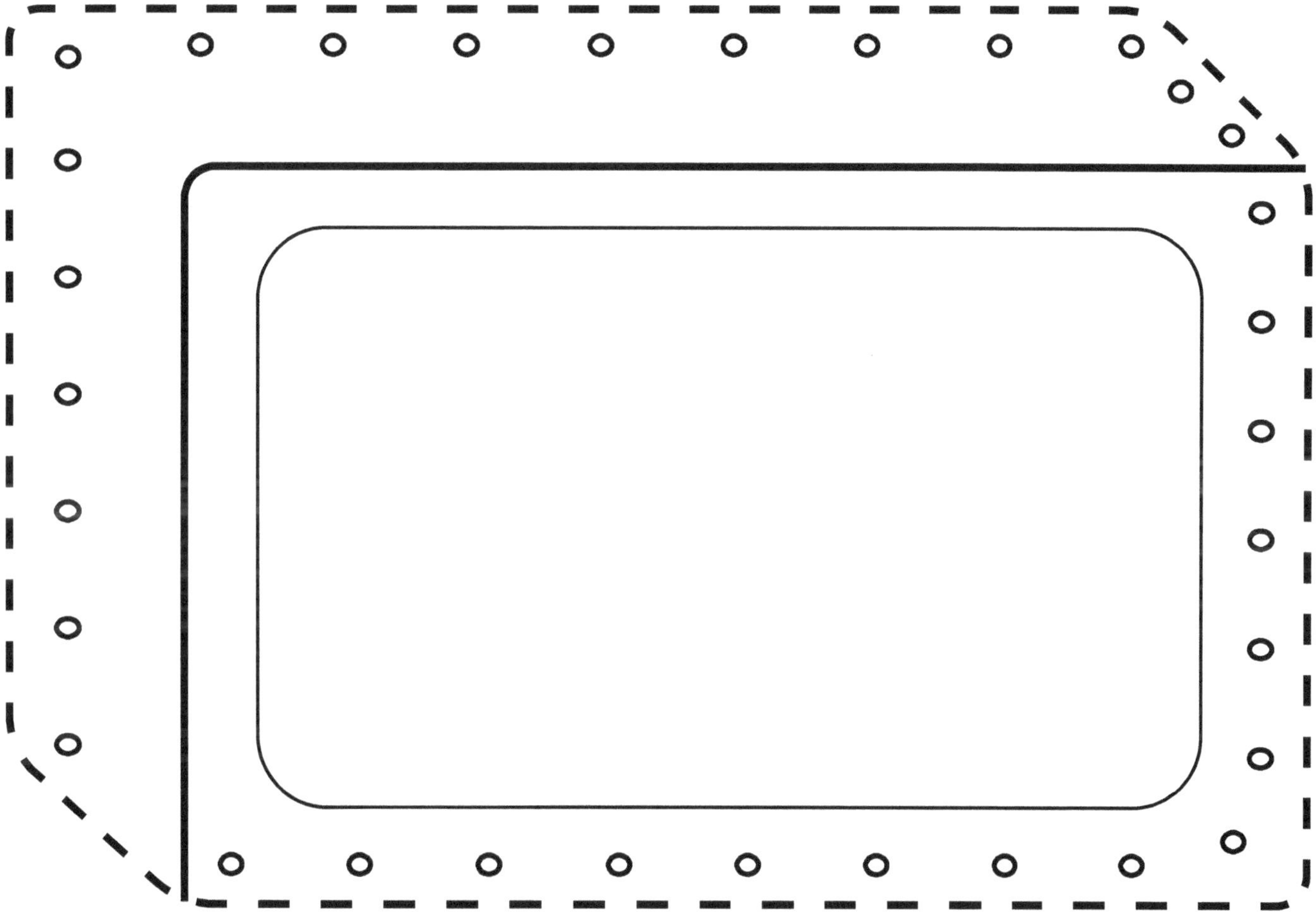

Extended Activity: *Make more frames using big, colored pictures from magazines and newspapers for the children to practice lacing.*

I got a/an ... **today!**

(To the teacher: Encircle the hand gesture that best describes how the child worked on this activity.)

 - fairly well  - well  - very well

____

Teacher's Signature

Tearing Activity

ACTIVITY 4

Guide: Have the children tear along the straight lines to make strips of paper. Let them paste the shaded paper strips onto an oslo paper to make a beautiful collage.

Extended Activity: *Have the children count the paper strips before the pasting activity. Review with them the numerals one to nine.*

I got a/an    **today!**

(To the teacher: Encircle the hand gesture that best describes how the child worked on this activity.)

 - fairly well  - well  - very well

____
Teacher's Signature

Guide: Have the children tear along the slant lines to make strips of paper. Let them paste the shaded paper strips onto one-half page of newspaper to make a beautiful collage.

Extended Activity: *Have the children add trimmings to their collage. Review with them the triangle shape and the numerals one to eight.*

I got a/an    **today!**

(To the teacher: Encircle the hand gesture that best describes how the child worked on this activity.)

 - fairly well  - well  - very well

____
Teacher's Signature

Guide: Have the children tear along the wavy lines to make strips of paper. Let them paste the shaded paper strips onto a large, empty softdrink bottle to make a beautiful piece of art.

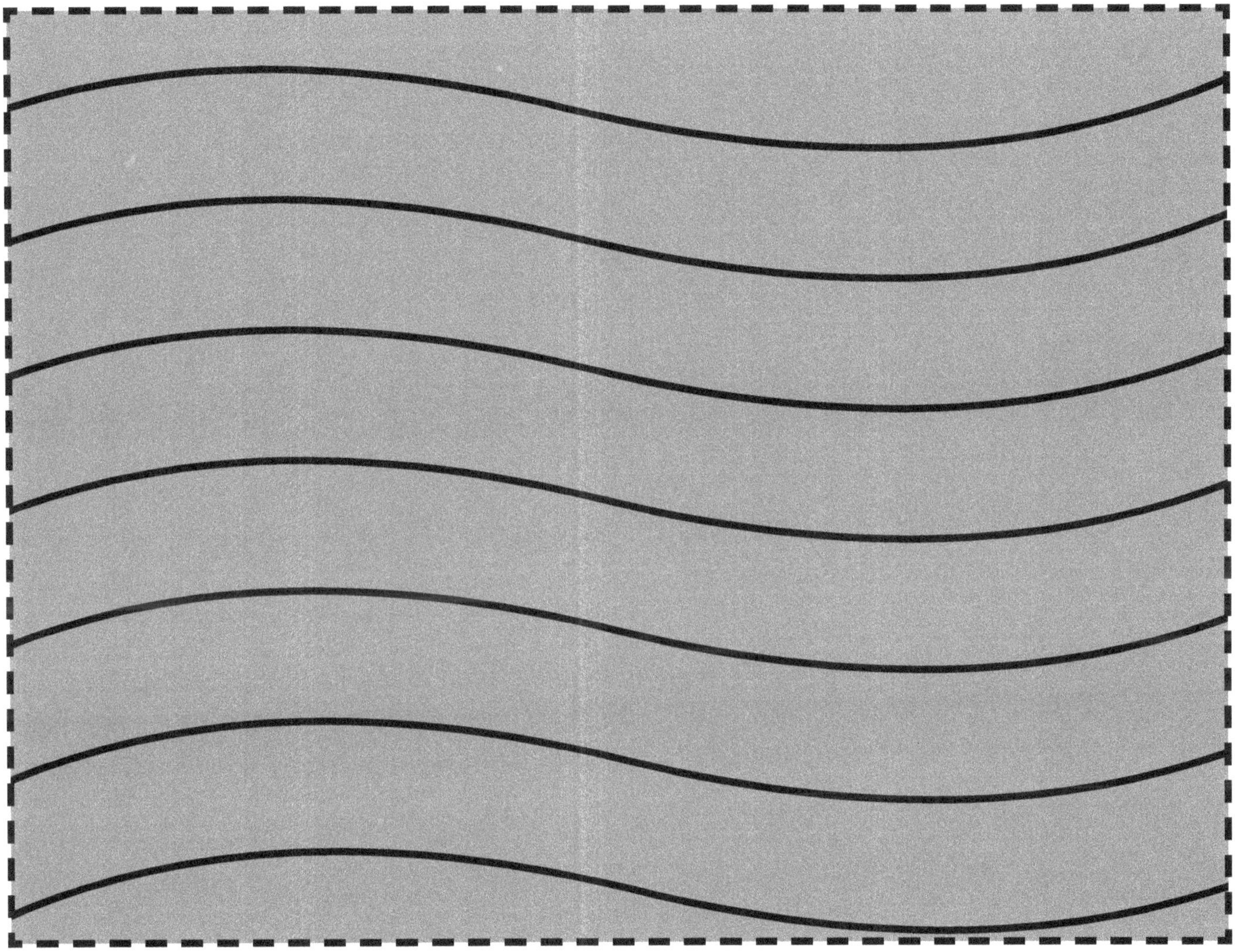

Extended Activity: *Have the children add trimmings to the decorated bottle. Review with them the numerals one to six and the concept of straight and curved lines.*

I got a/an    **today!**

(To the teacher: Encircle the hand gesture that best describes how the child worked on this activity.)

 - fairly well  - well  - very well

____

Teacher's Signature

Cutting Activity

ACTIVITY 7

Guide: Let the children cut along the straight lines to make strips of paper. Let them paste the shaded paper strips onto a paper plate to make a beautiful work of art.

Extended Activity: *Have the children add different materials to the paper plate to make a beautiful design. Review with them the numerals one to nine.*

I got a/an    **today!**

(To the teacher: Encircle the hand gesture that best describes how the child worked on this activity.)

 - fairly well  - well  - very well

____

Teacher's Signature

Guide: Let the children cut along the slant lines to make strips of paper. Let them paste the shaded paper strips onto a shoebox to make a unique chest.

Extended Activity: *Have the children add trimmings to the shoebox. Review with them the numerals one to eight.*

I got a/an    **today!**

(To the teacher: Encircle the hand gesture that best describes how the child worked on this activity.)

 - fairly well  - well  - very well

Teacher's Signature

Guide: Let the children cut along the wavy lines to make strips of paper. Let them paste the shaded paper strips onto one-half page of newspaper to make a fabulous collage.

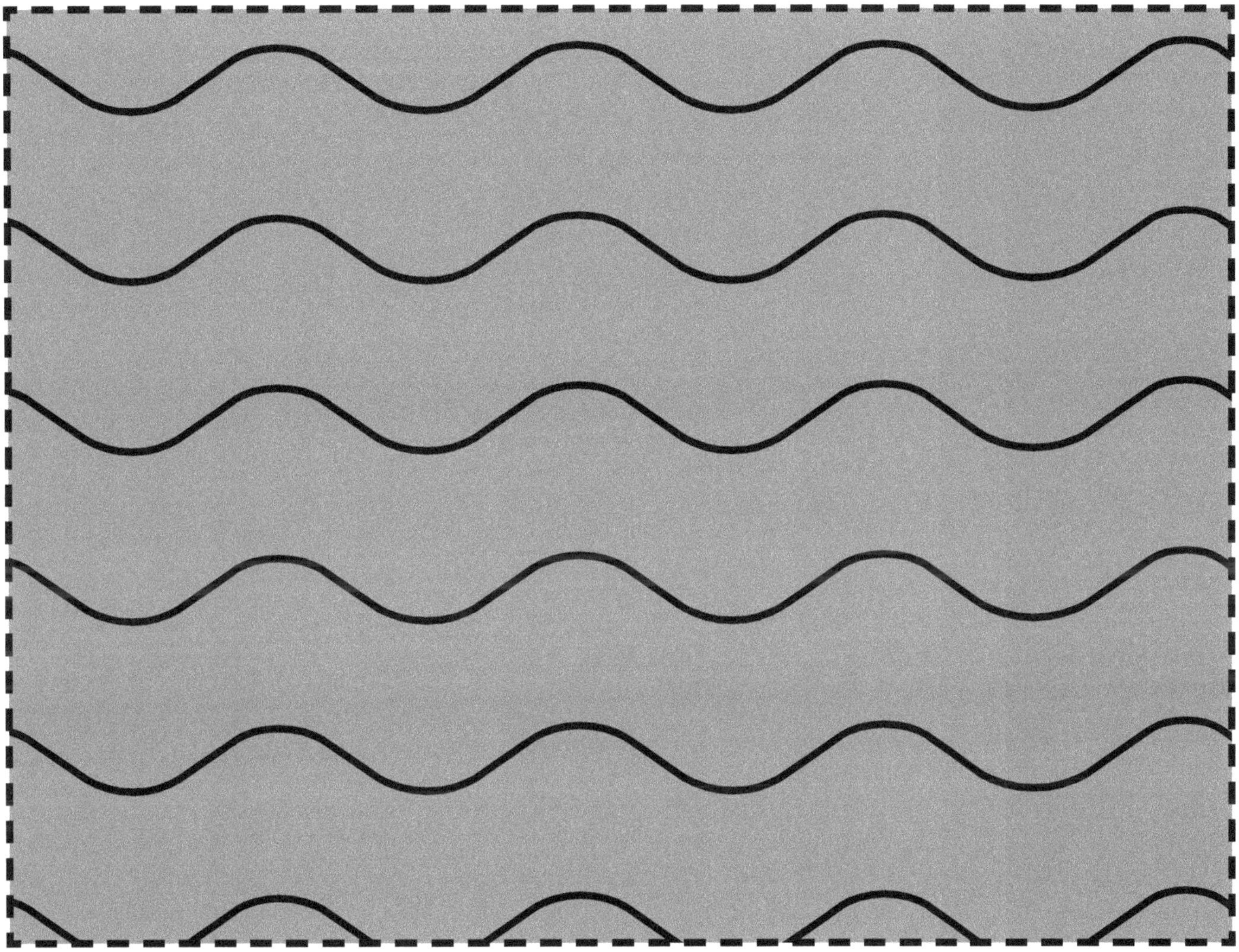

Extended Activity: *Have the children add different trimmings to the collage. Review with them the concept of wavy lines.*

I got a/an    **today!**

(To the teacher: Encircle the hand gesture that best describes how the child worked on this activity.)

 - fairly well  - well  - very well

____
Teacher's Signature

Guide: Have the children cut along the short and long straight lines to make strips of paper. Let them paste the shaded strips onto a big tin can to make a beautiful piece of art.

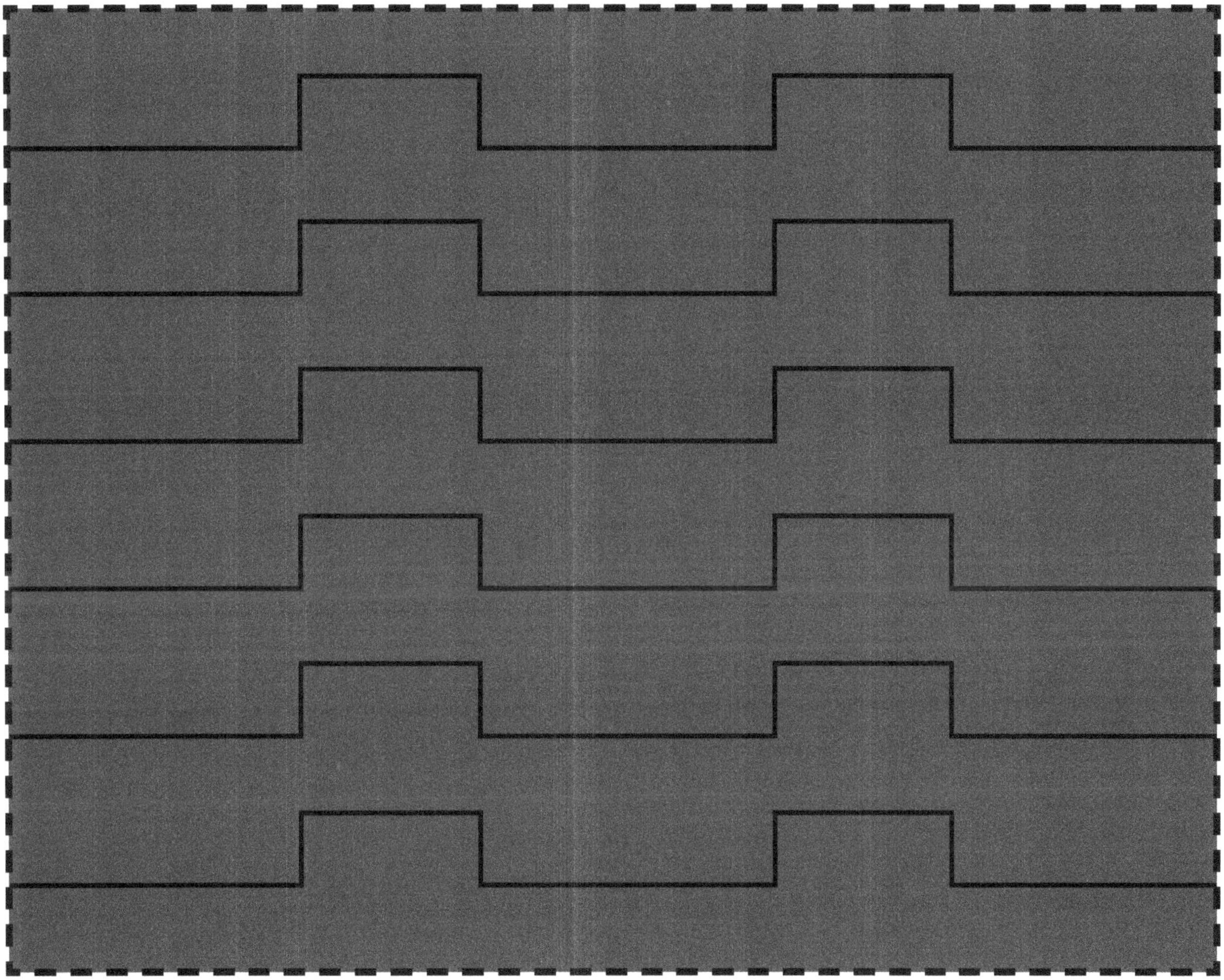

Extended Activity: *Have the children add trimmings to the tin can. Review with them the concept of long and short.*

I got a/an    **today!**

(To the teacher: Encircle the hand gesture that best describes how the child worked on this activity.)

 - fairly well  - well  - very well

____
Teacher's Signature

ACTIVITY 11

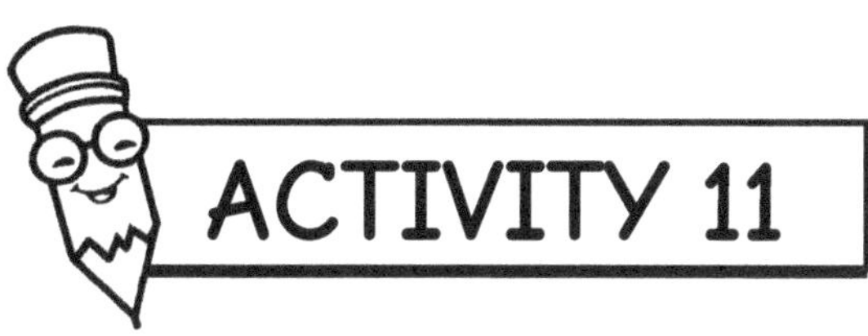

Guide: Have the children cut along the short and long slant lines to make strips of paper. Let them paste the shaded paper strips onto a big plastic container to make a colorful chest.

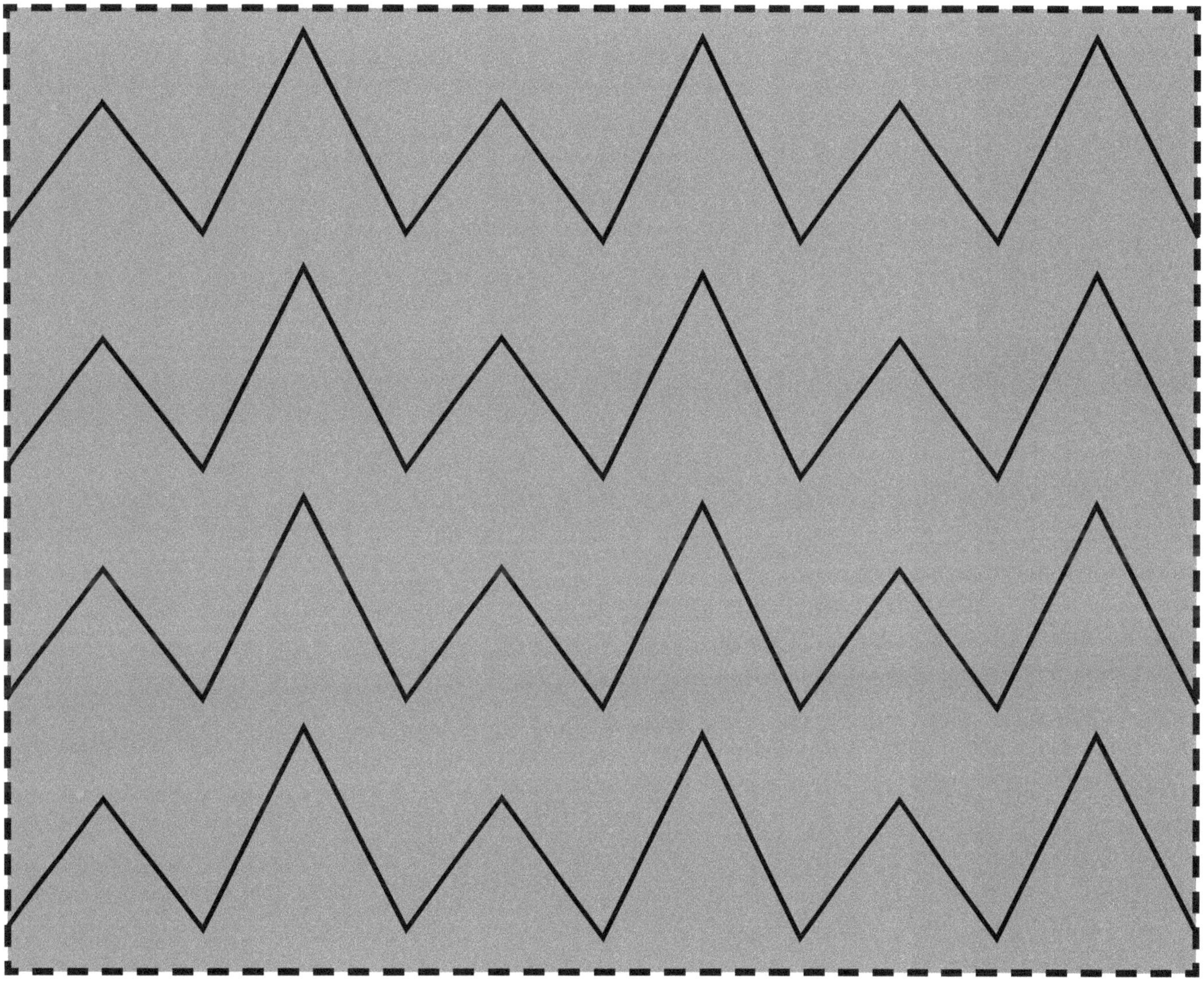

Extended Activity: *Have the children add trimmings to the plastic container. Review with them the concept of long and short.*

I got a/an   **today!**

(To the teacher: Encircle the hand gesture that best describes how the child worked on this activity.)

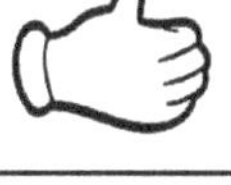

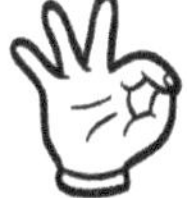

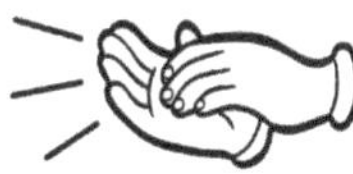

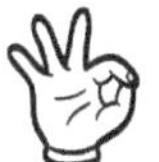

 - fairly well - well - very well

____

Teacher's Signature

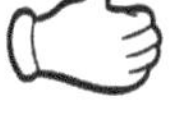

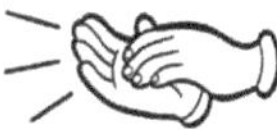

Clipping Activity

ACTIVITY 12

Guide: Have the children color the objects on each picture and number card. Cut out the frames and glue them onto used folders. (You may assign this as Home Activity.) Ask the children to count the objects on the cards and then put a clothespin on the correct numeral.

3 5 8

6 1 4

8 5 10

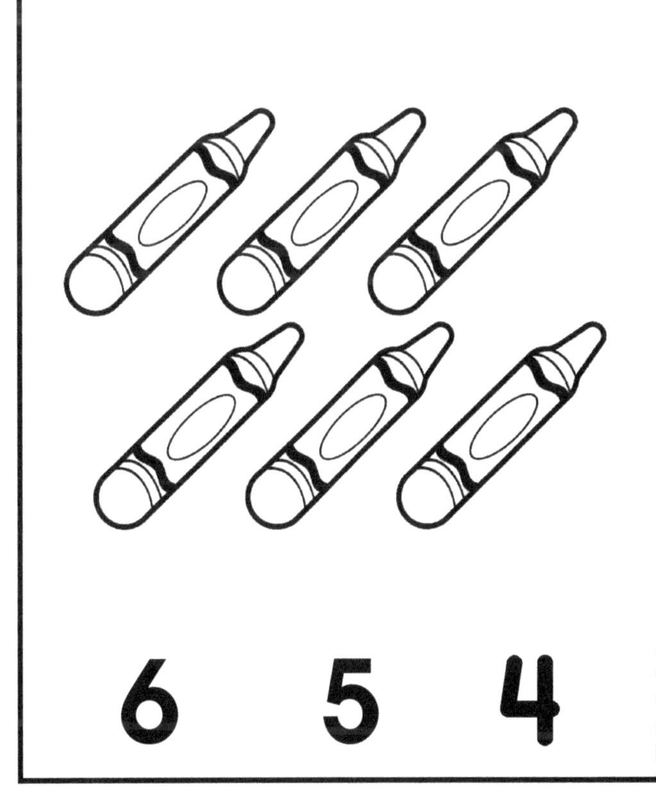
6 5 4

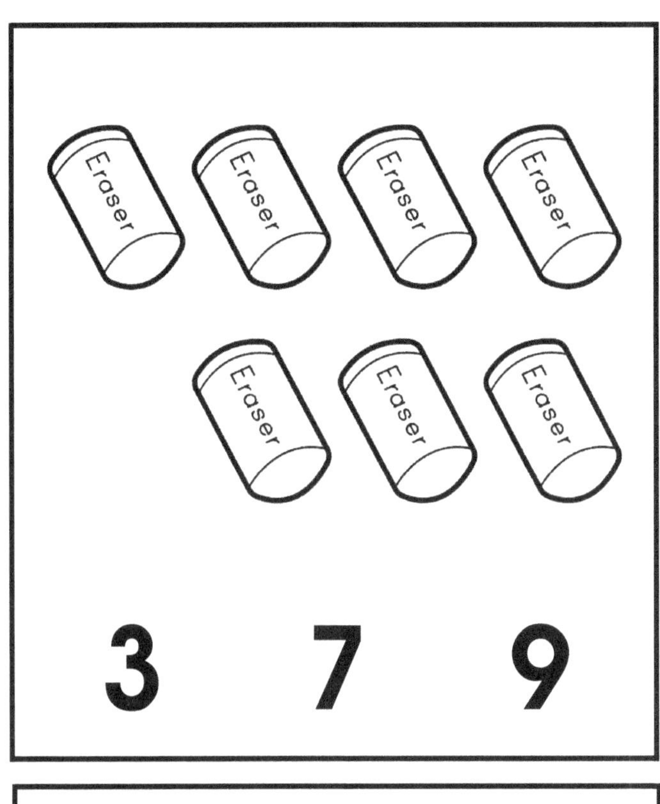

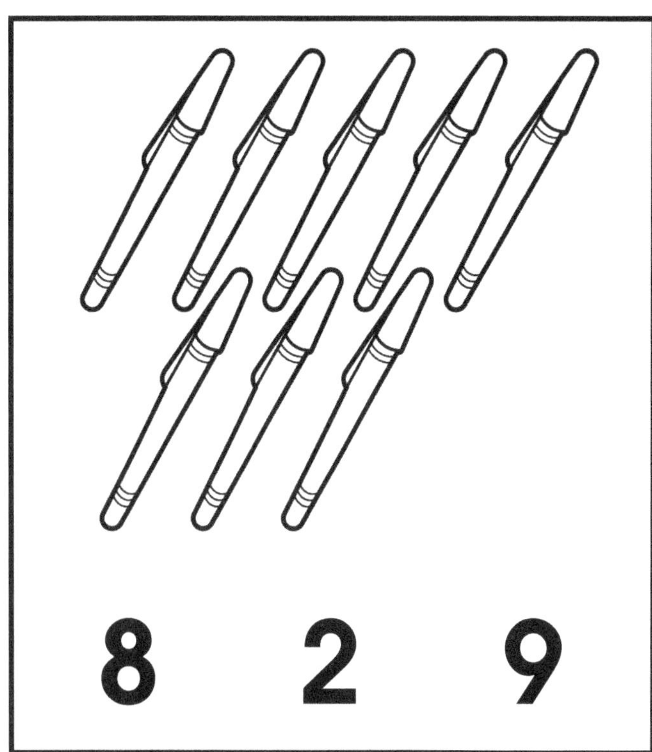

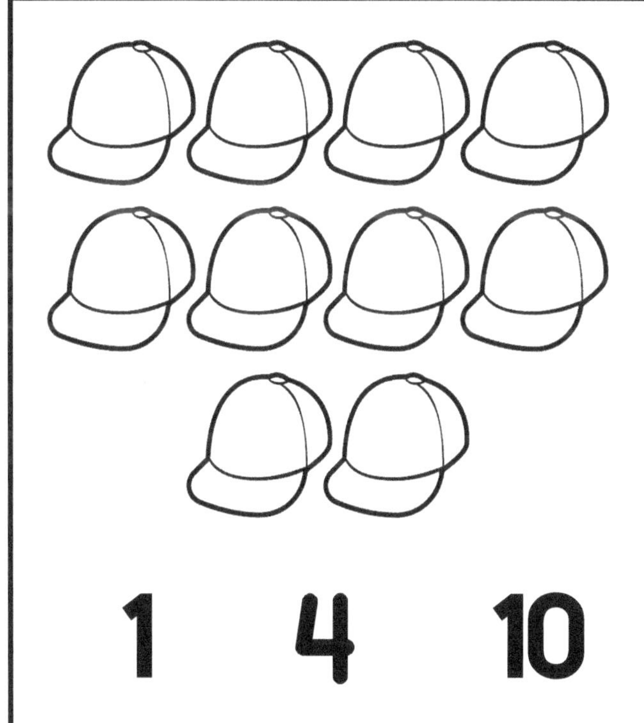

(To the teacher: Encircle the hand gesture that best describes how the child worked on this activity.)

- very well

____

Teacher's Signature

THE BASIC WRITING STROKES

Guide: Demonstrate how to properly grip the pencil between the thumb and pointer finger, letting the pencil rest on the middle finger.

These are the basic strokes that we use in writing.

HORIZONTAL LINES

VERTICAL LINES

RIGHT SLANTS

LEFT SLANTS

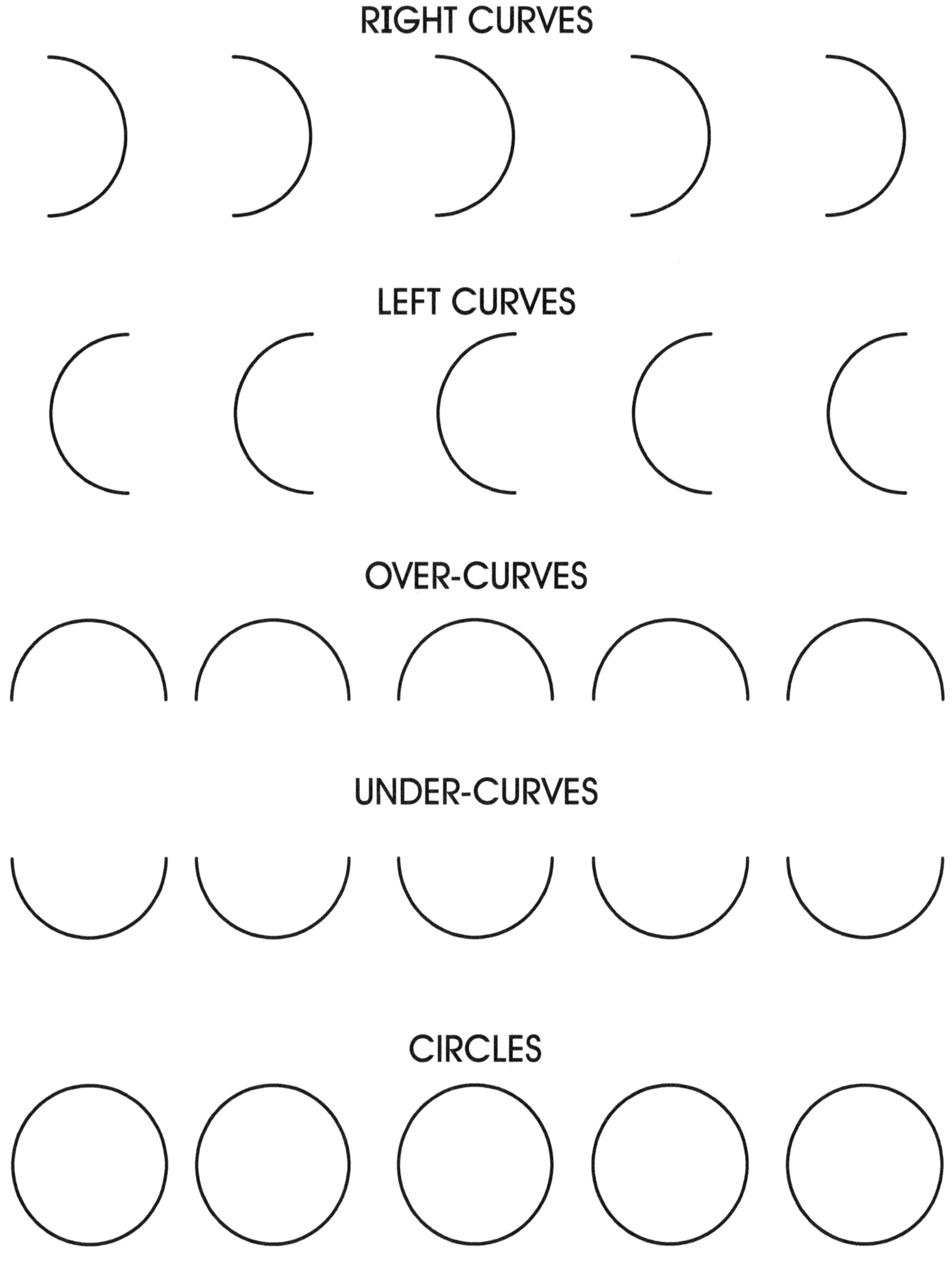
RIGHT CURVES
LEFT CURVES
OVER-CURVES
UNDER-CURVES
CIRCLES

Make horizontal lines by tracing the broken lines. Follow the left-to-right movement.

Draw more horizontal lines. Make five sets in each row. Start from left to right.

I got a/an ... **today!**

(To the teacher: Encircle the hand gesture that best describes how the child worked on this activity.)

- fairly well
- well
- very well

Teacher's Signature

Make vertical lines by tracing the broken lines. Follow the up-down movement.

Draw more vertical lines. Make seven sets in each row. Start from top to bottom.

I got a/an today!

(To the teacher: Encircle the hand gesture that best describes how the child worked on this activity.)

- fairly well - well - very well

Teacher's Signature

Make right slants by tracing the broken lines. Follow the up-down right slant movement.

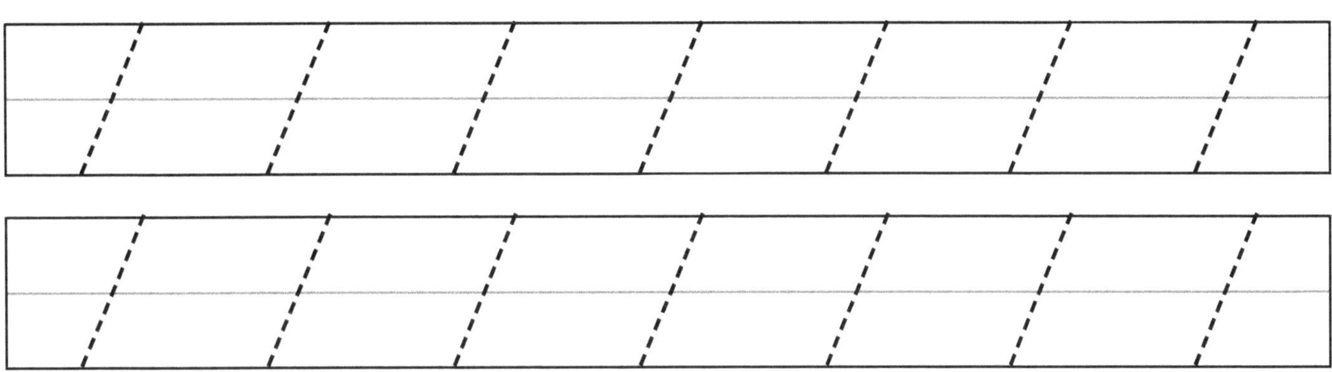

Draw more right slants. Make seven sets in each row. Start from top to bottom.

I got a/an    **today!**

(To the teacher: Encircle the hand gesture that best describes how the child worked on this activity.)

 - fairly well  - well  - very well

____

Teacher's Signature

Make left slants by tracing the broken lines. Follow the up-down left slant movement.

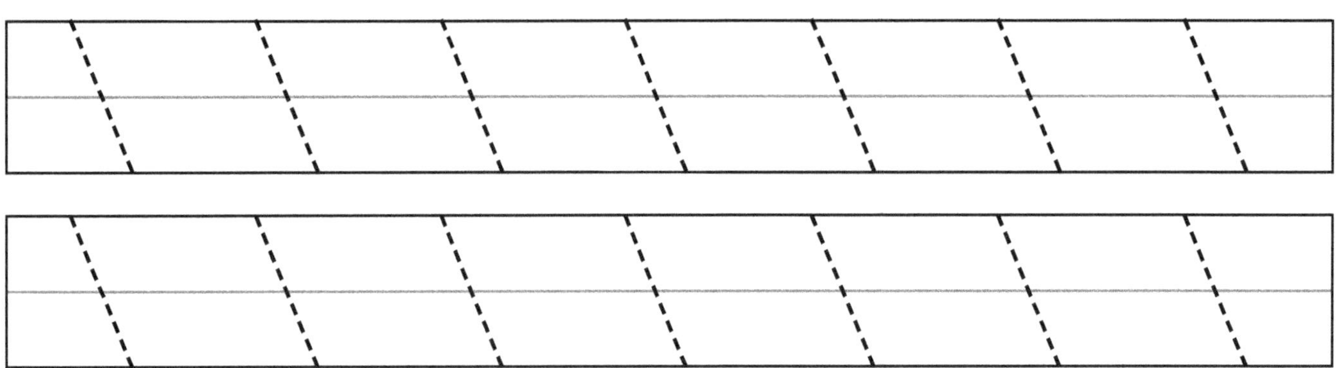

Draw more left slants. Make seven sets in each row. Start from top to bottom.

I got a/an    **today!**

(To the teacher: Encircle the hand gesture that best describes how the child worked on this activity.)

 - fairly well  - well  - very well

____
Teacher's Signature

Make right curves by tracing the broken lines. Follow the up-down right curve movement.

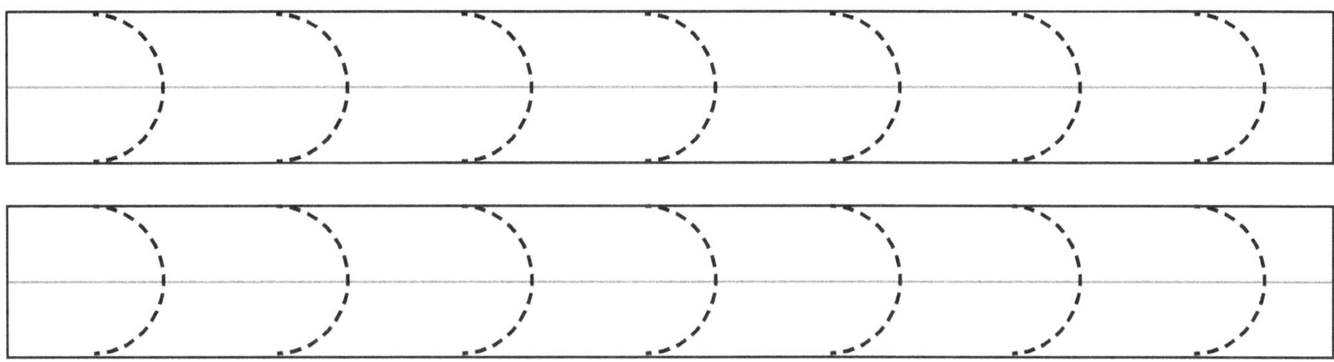

Draw more right curves. Make seven sets in each row. Start from top to bottom.

I got a/an    **today!**

(To the teacher: Encircle the hand gesture that best describes how the child worked on this activity.)

 - fairly well  - well  - very well

Teacher's Signature

Make left curves by tracing the broken lines. Follow the up-down left curve movement.

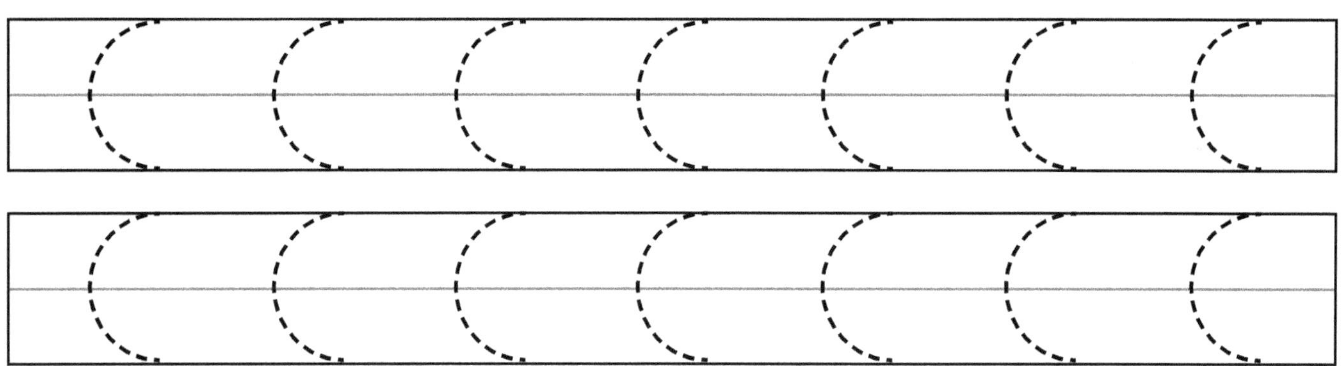

Draw more left curves. Make seven sets in each row. Start from top to bottom.

I got a/an    **today!**

(To the teacher: Encircle the hand gesture that best describes how the child worked on this activity.)

 - fairly well  - well  - very well

____
Teacher's Signature

Make over-curves by tracing the broken lines. Follow the left-to-right over-curve movement.

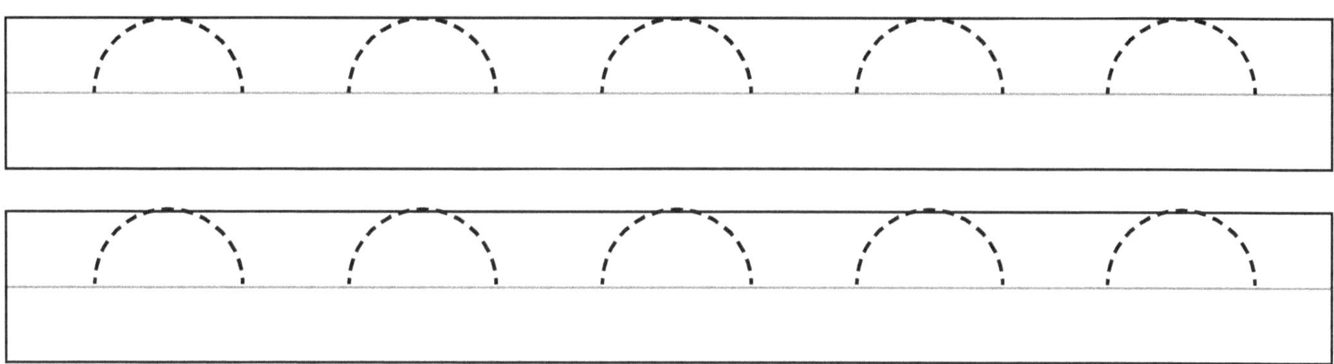

Draw more over-curves. Make five sets in each row. Start from left to right.

I got a/an    **today!**

(To the teacher: Encircle the hand gesture that best describes how the child worked on this activity.)

 - fairly well  - well  - very well

____

Teacher's Signature

ACTIVITY 20

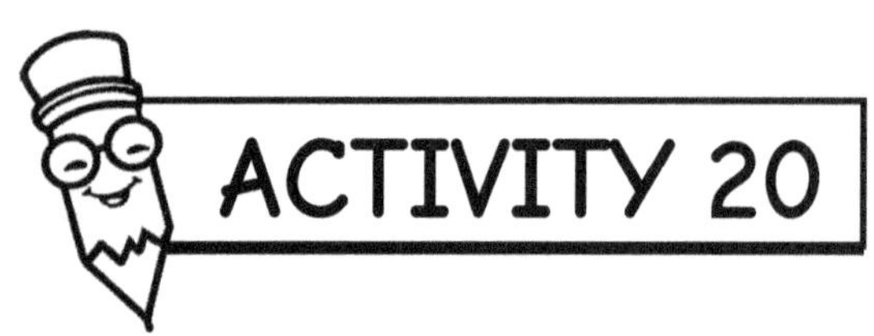

Make under-curves by tracing the broken lines. Follow the left-to-right under-curve movement.

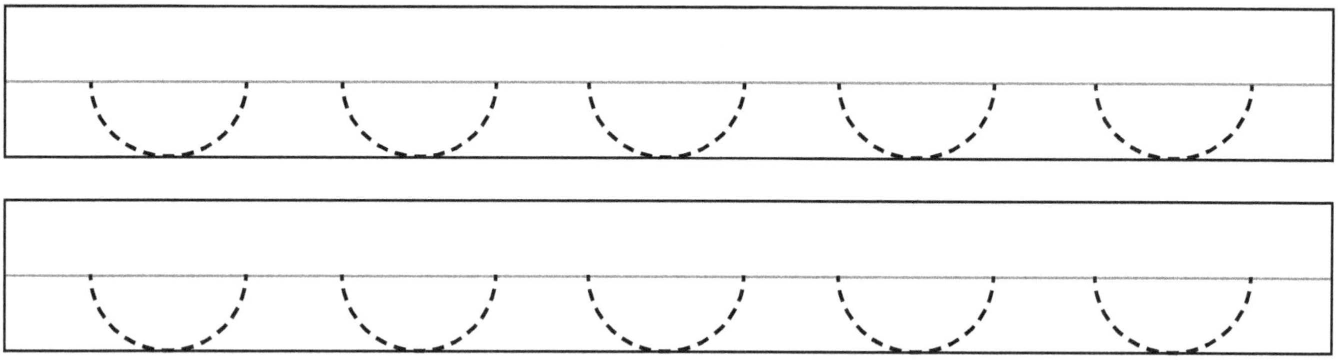

Draw more under-curves. Make five sets in each row. Start from left to right.

I got a/an   **today!**

(To the teacher: Encircle the hand gesture that best describes how the child worked on this activity.)

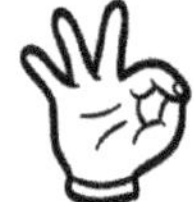

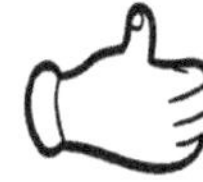

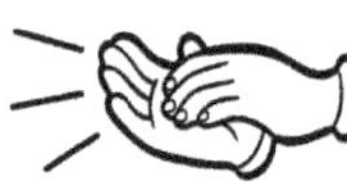

 - fairly well - well - very well

____

Teacher's Signature

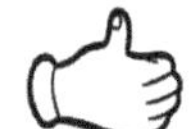

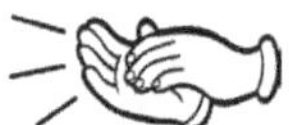

Make circles by tracing the broken lines. Follow the circular movement.

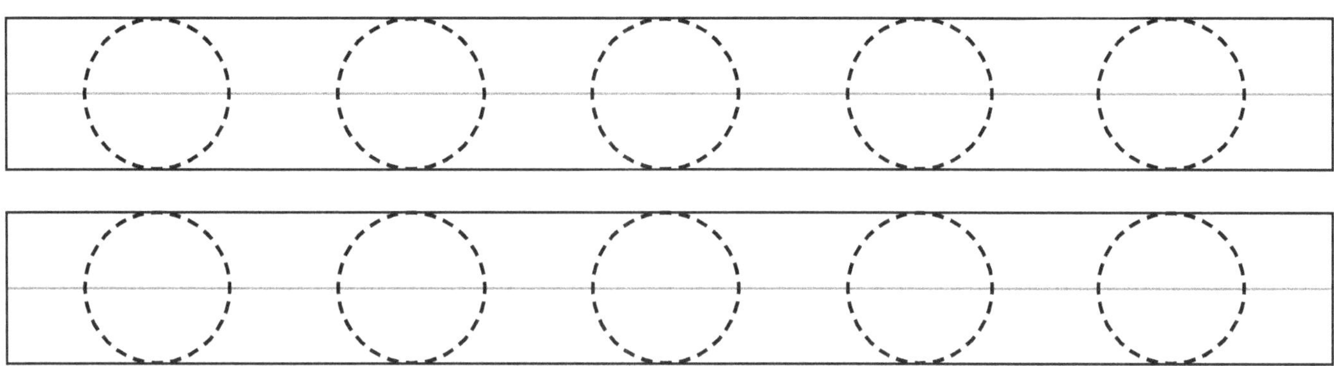

Draw more circles. Make five sets in each row. Follow the circular movement.

I got a/an    **today!**

(To the teacher: Encircle the hand gesture that best describes how the child worked on this activity.)

 - fairly well  - well  - very well

____

Teacher's Signature

ACTIVITY 22

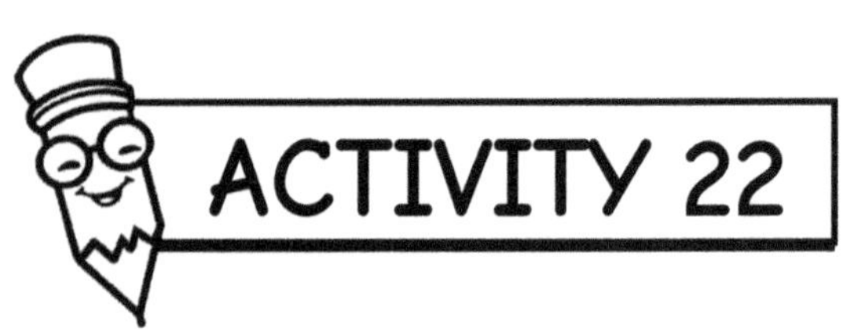

Trace the following shapes.

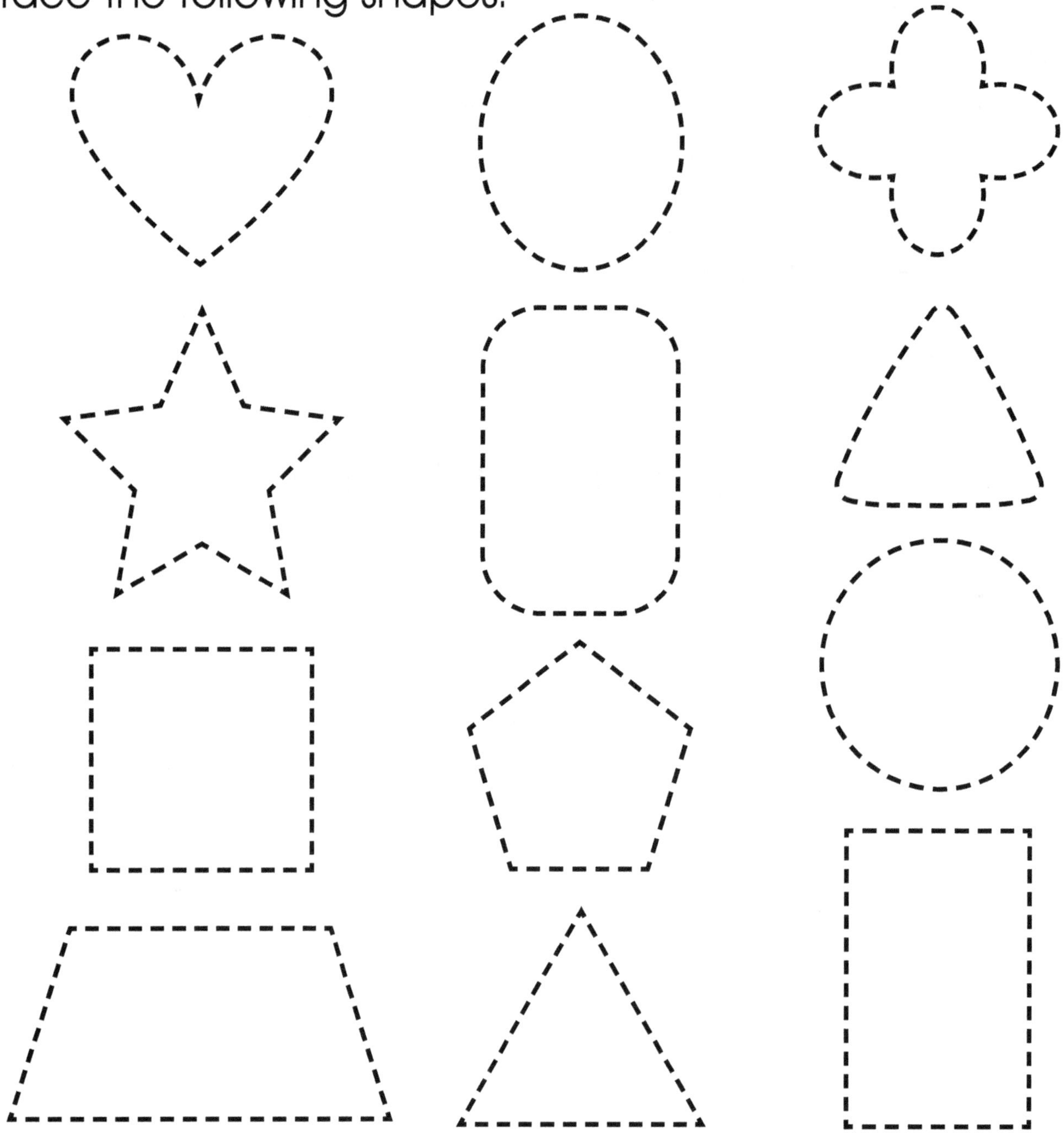

I got a/an	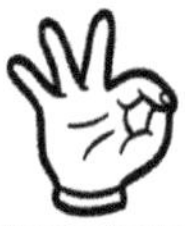	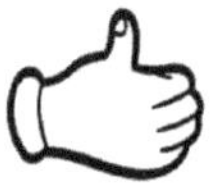	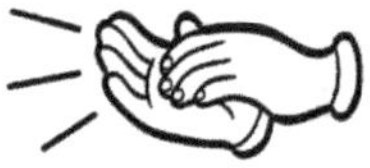	**today!**

(To the teacher: Encircle the hand gesture that best describes how the child worked on this activity.)

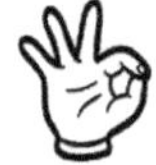

 - fairly well - well - very well

____

Teacher's Signature

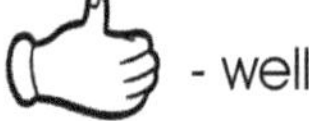

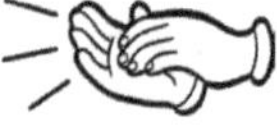

LESSON 3 THE WRITING INSETS

Guide: Make writing insets of different shapes out of wood or illustration board. Have the children touch the edge of each inset. Have them trace the insets on bond paper to practice control and grip.

These are writing insets. Exercises with these materials will help you refine pencil control and help you make even spaces in writing.

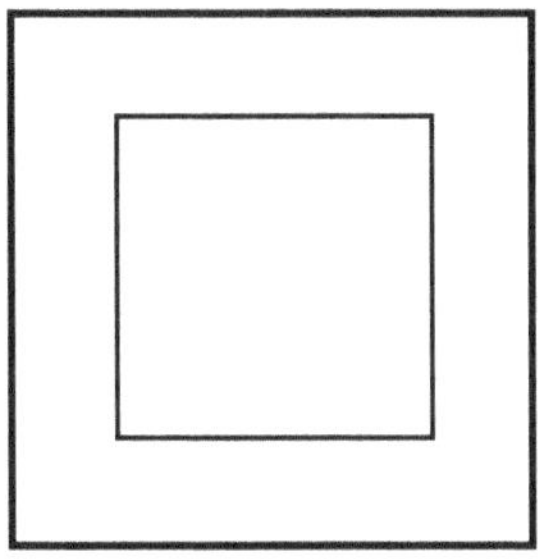

square 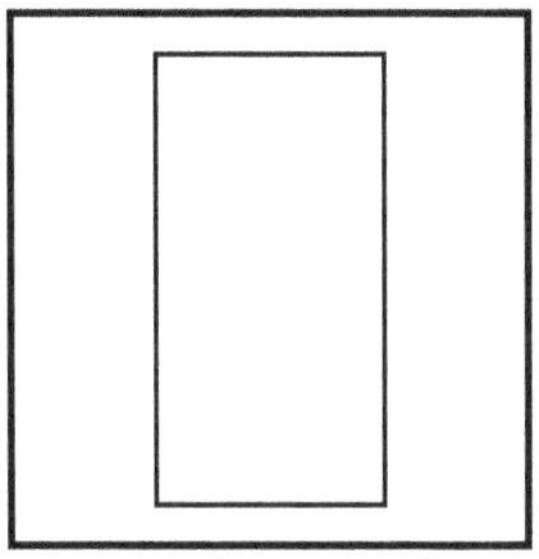 rectangle 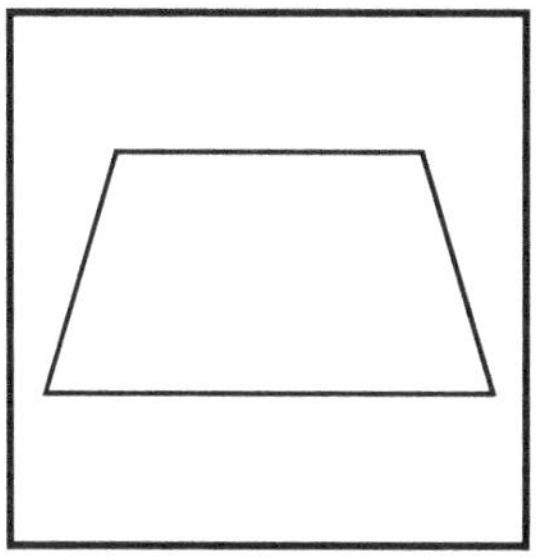 trapezoid

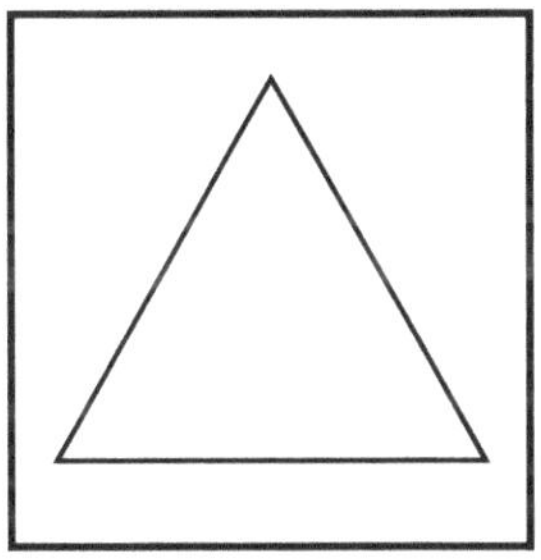

triangle 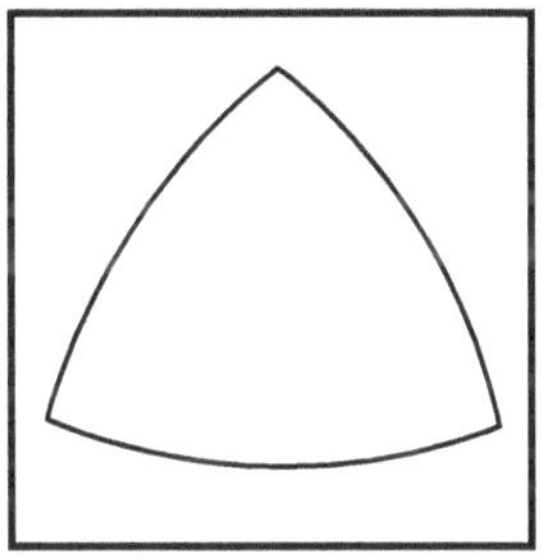 curved triangle 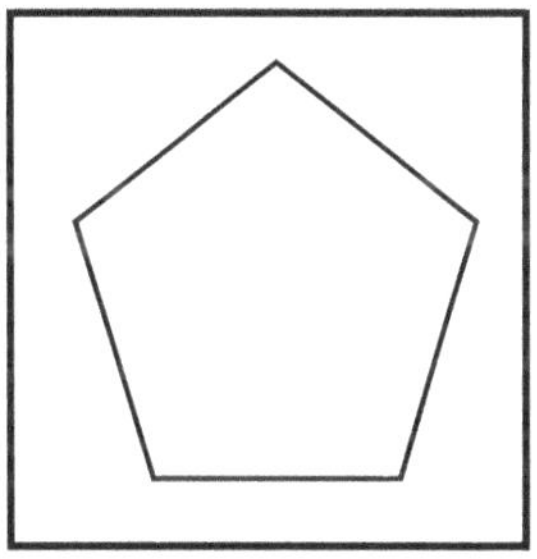 pentagon  quatrefoil

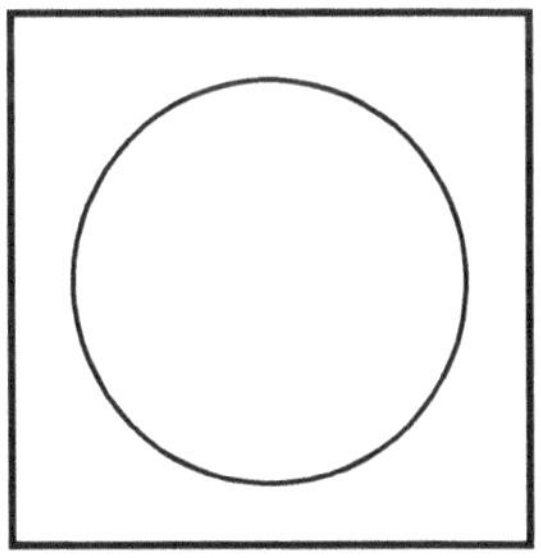

circle 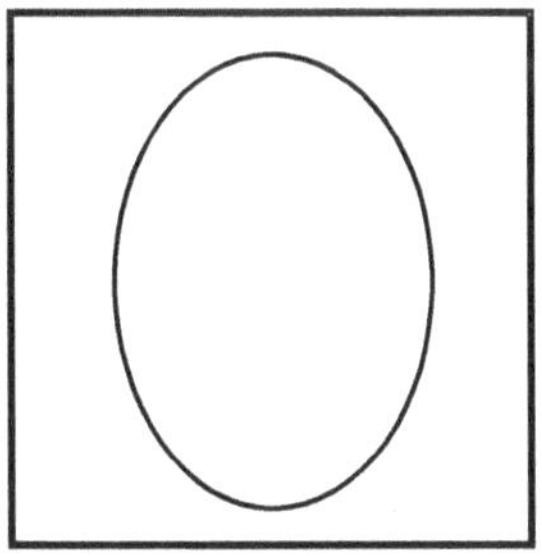 ellipse 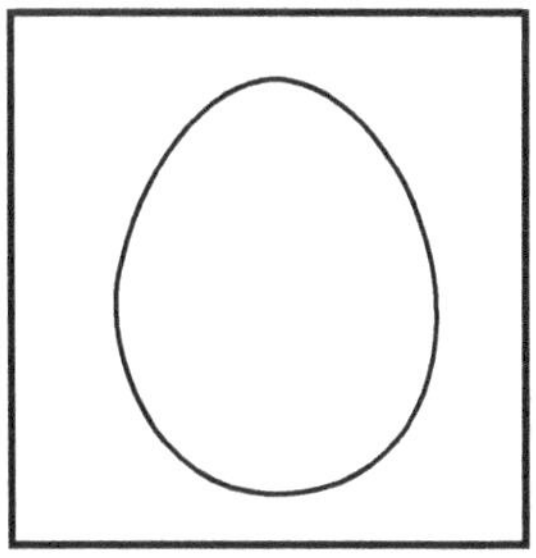 oval 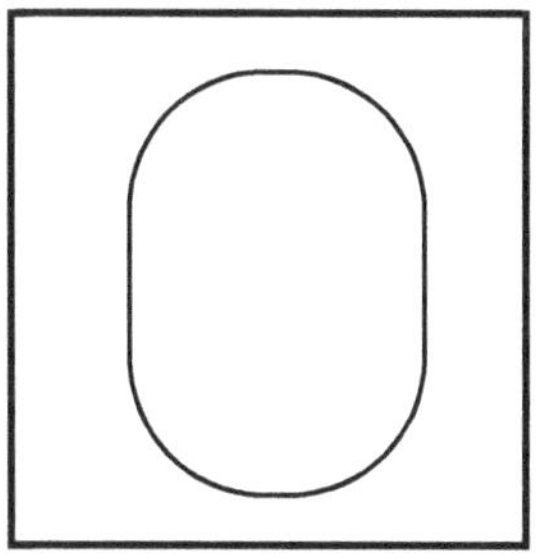 oblong

I got a/an    **today!**

(To the teacher: Encircle the hand gesture that best describes how the child worked on this activity.)

 - fairly well  - well 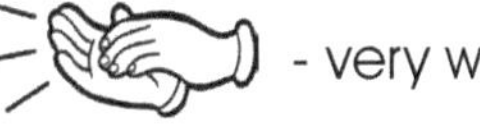 - very well

____
Teacher's Signature

Using red and blue colored pencils, fill the shapes with horizontal and vertical lines. Put equal spaces between the lines. Do not write outside the shapes. Follow the given examples.

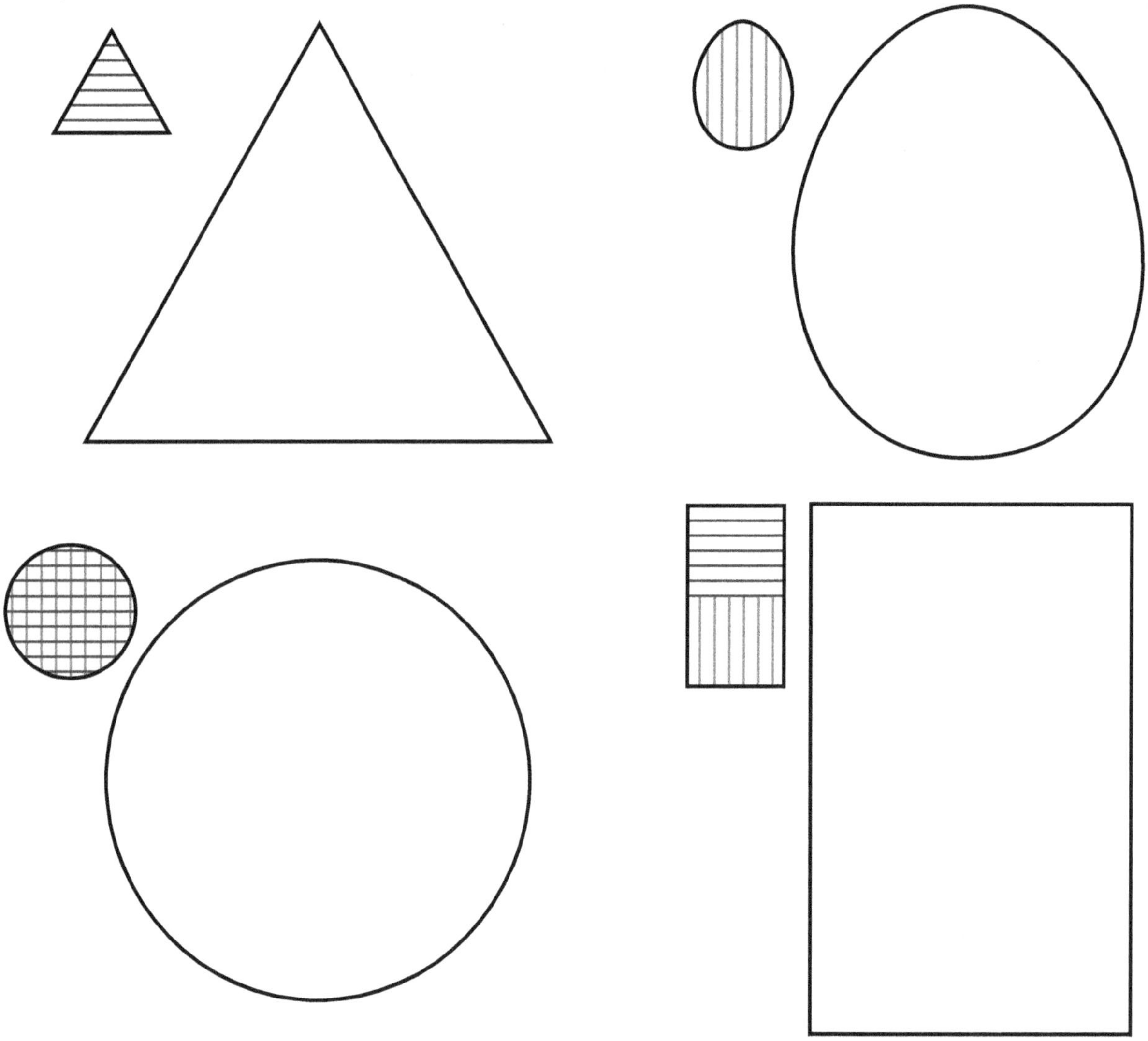

I got a/an 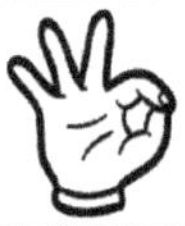 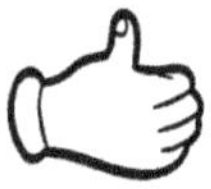 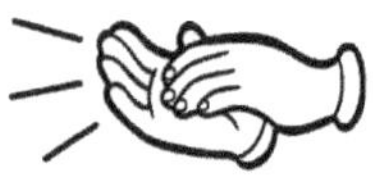 ... today!

(To the teacher: Encircle the hand gesture that best describes how the child worked on this activity.)

 - fairly well  - well  - very well

____

Teacher's Signature

Using red and blue colored pencils, fill the shapes with right and left slants. Put equal spaces between the lines. Do not write outside the shapes. Follow the given examples.

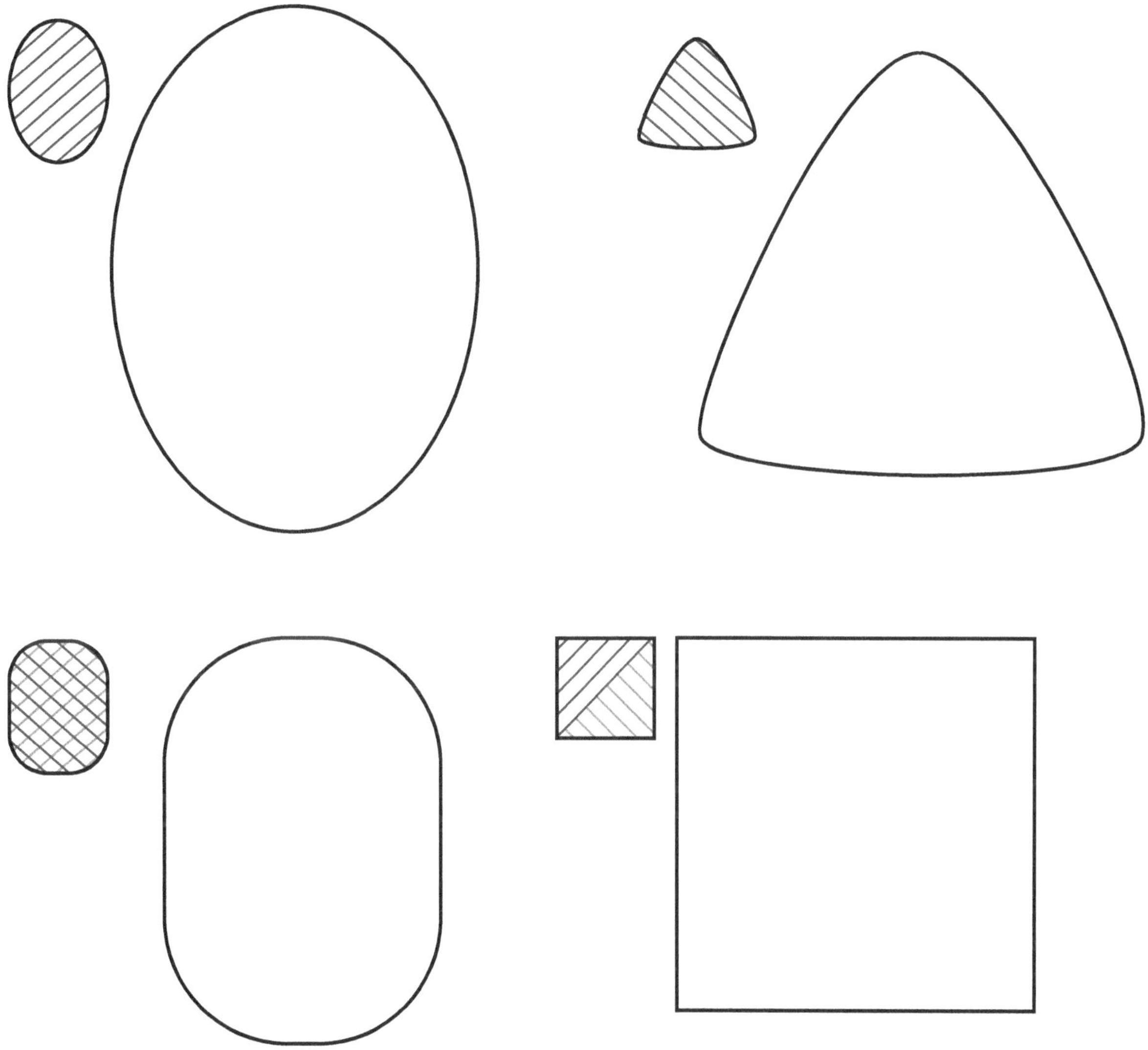

I got a/an 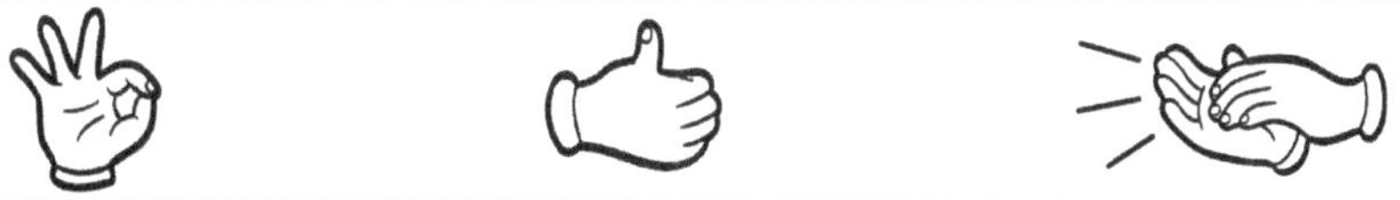 today!

(To the teacher: Encircle the hand gesture that best describes how the child worked on this activity.)

- very well

Teacher's Signature

ACTIVITY 25

Using red and blue colored pencils, fill the shapes with horizontal, vertical, and slant lines. Put equal spaces between the lines. Do not write outside the shapes. Follow the given examples.

I got a/an  ... today!

(To the teacher: Encircle the hand gesture that best describes how the child worked on this activity.)

- fairly well  - well  - very well

____
Teacher's Signature

THE LETTERS OF THE ALPHABET

Letter **Aa**

This is the proper way to write the letter **Aa**.

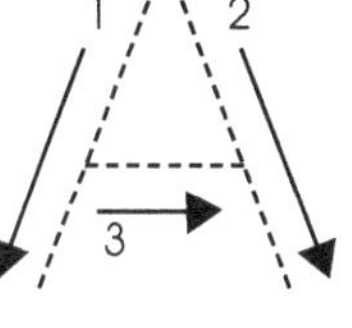

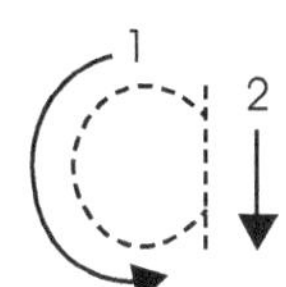

Practice writing the letter **Aa** by tracing the broken lines. Follow the direction of the arrows.

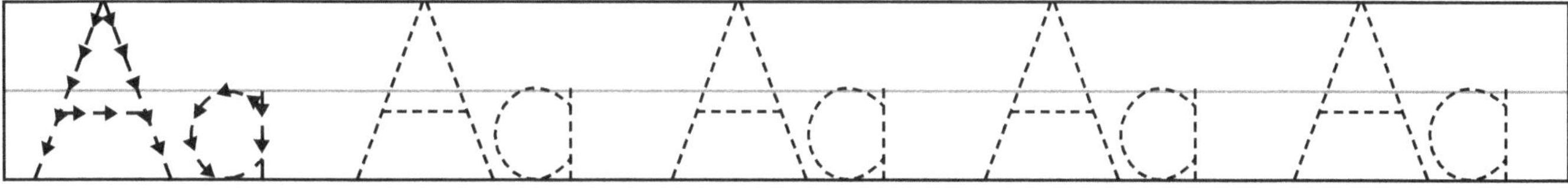

Write more letter **Aa's**. Make five sets. Leave equal spaces between the letter pairs.

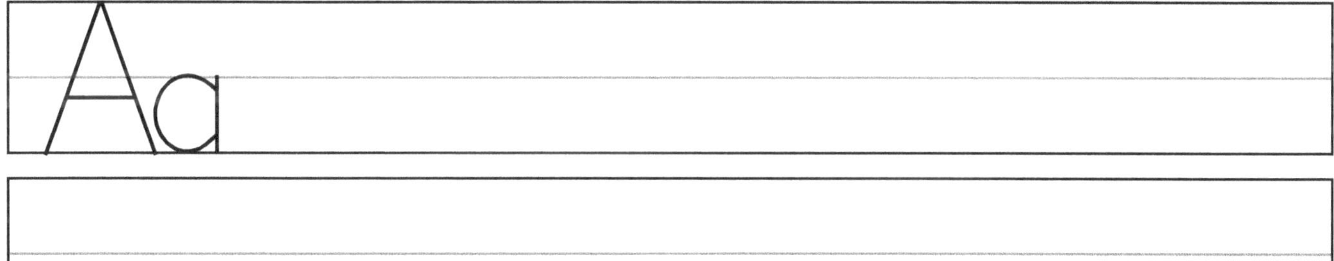

Write the letter **a** where you hear its sound.

I got a/an   **today!**

(To the teacher: Encircle the hand gesture that best describes how the child worked on this activity.)

 - fairly well  - well  - very well

____
Teacher's Signature

Letter **Bb**

This is the proper way to write the letter **Bb**.

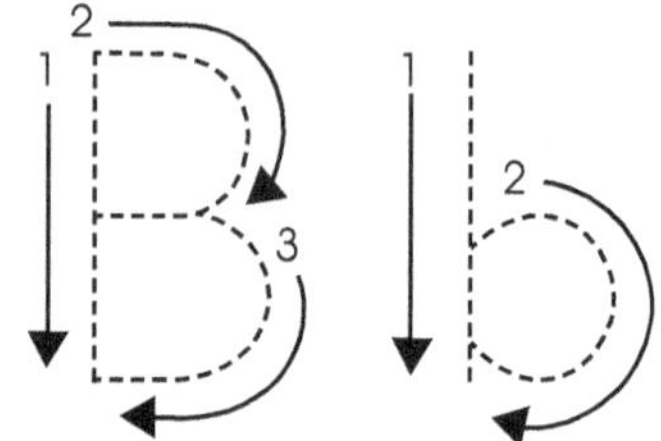

ACTIVITY 27

Practice writing the letter **Bb** by tracing the broken lines. Follow the direction of the arrows.

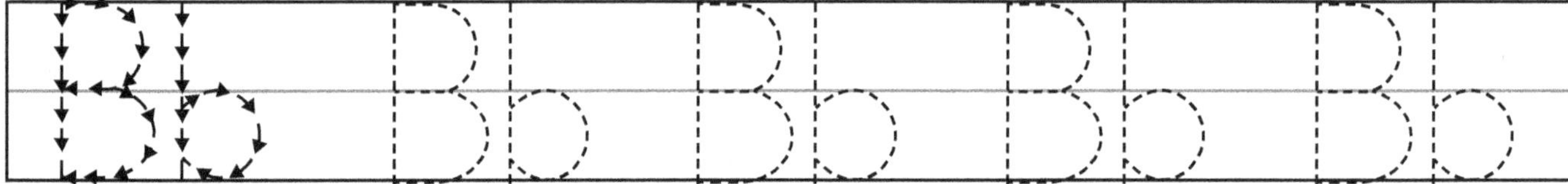

Write more letter **Bb's**. Make five sets. Leave equal spaces between the letter pairs.

Write the letter **b** where you hear its sound.

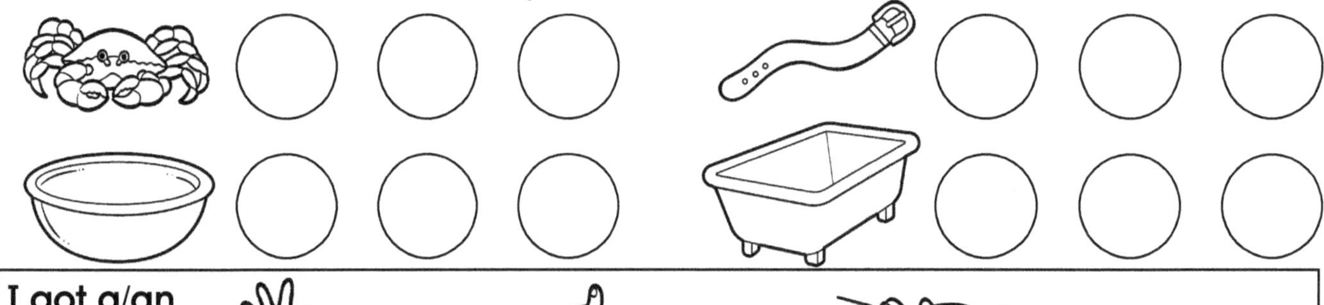

I got a/an    **today!**

(To the teacher: Encircle the hand gesture that best describes how the child worked on this activity.)

 - fairly well  - well  - very well

Teacher's Signature

Letter **<u>Cc</u>**

This is the proper way to write the letter **<u>Cc</u>**.

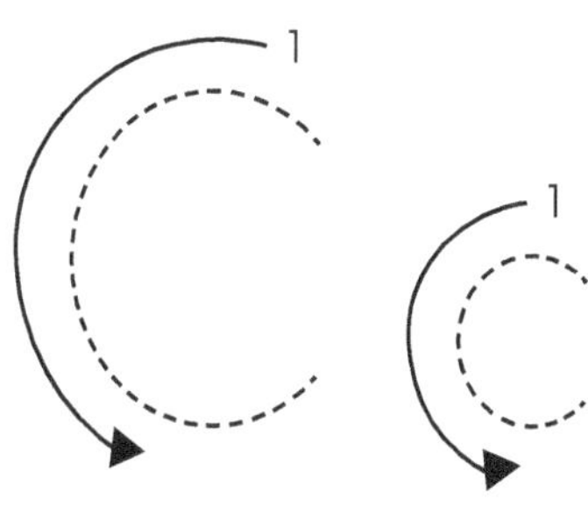

Practice writing the letter **<u>Cc</u>** by tracing the broken lines. Follow the direction of the arrows.

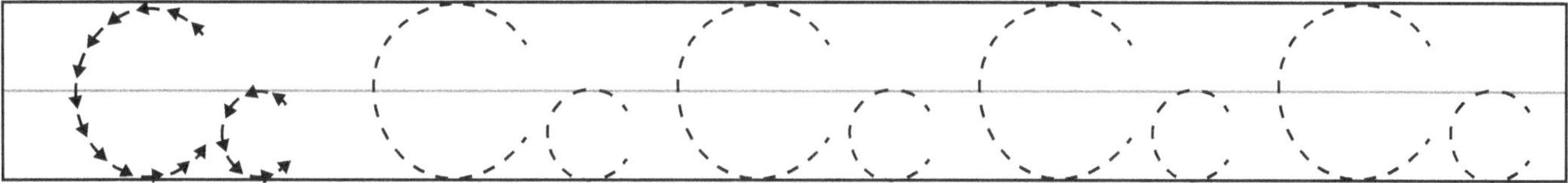

Write more letter **<u>Cc's</u>**. Make five sets. Leave equal spaces between the letter pairs.

Write the letter **<u>c</u>** where you hear its sound.

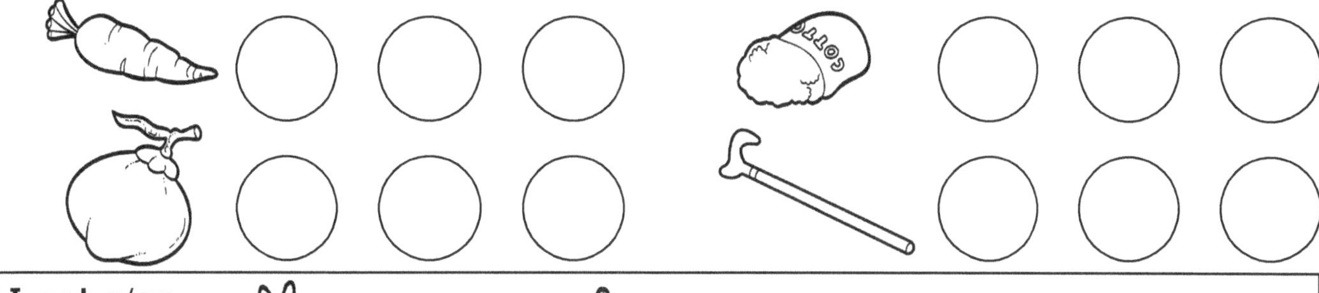

I got a/an   **today!**

(To the teacher: Encircle the hand gesture that best describes how the child worked on this activity.)

 - fairly well  - well  - very well

____
Teacher's Signature

Letter Dd

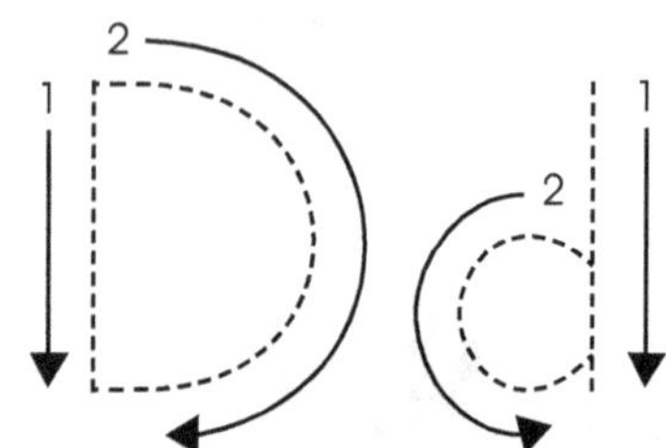

Practice writing the letter **Dd** by tracing the broken lines. Follow the direction of the arrows.

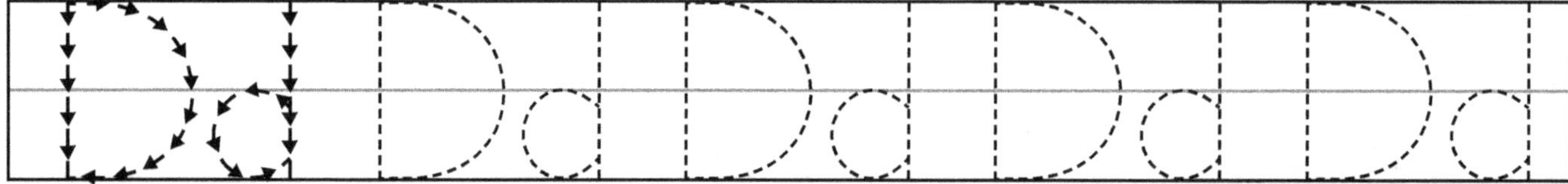

Write more letter **Dd's**. Make five sets. Leave equal spaces between the letter pairs.

Write the letter **d** where you hear its sound.

I got a/an ... today!

(To the teacher: Encircle the hand gesture that best describes how the child worked on this activity.)

 - fairly well  - well  - very well

____
Teacher's Signature

Letter Ee

This is the proper way to write the letter **Ee**.

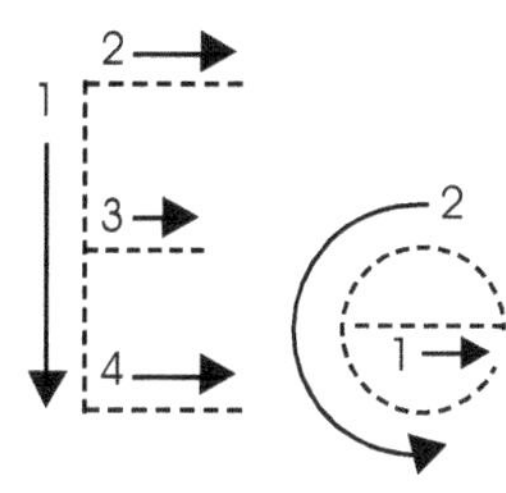

Practice writing the letter **Ee** by tracing the broken lines. Follow the direction of the arrows.

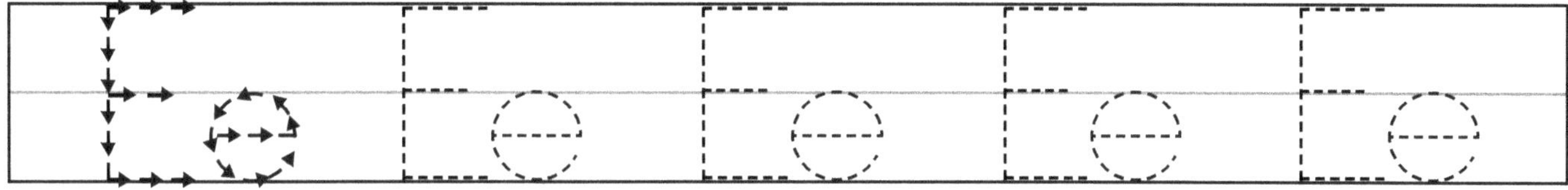

Write more letter **Ee's**. Make five sets. Leave equal spaces between the letter pairs.

Write the letter **e** where you hear its sound.

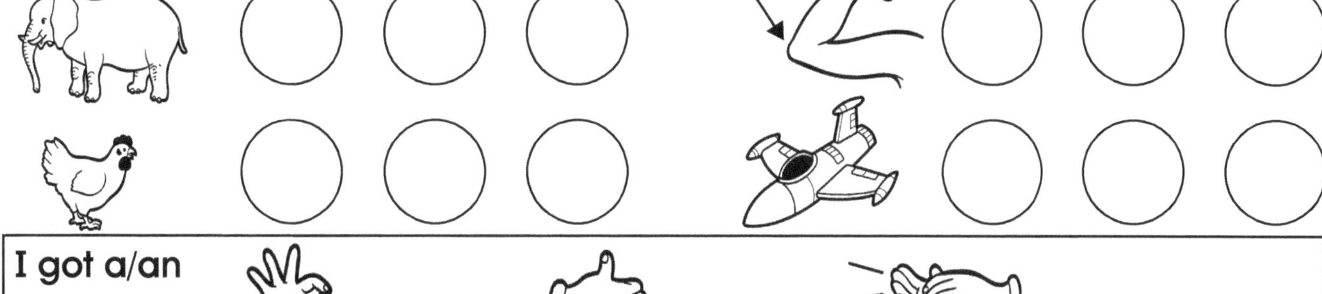

I got a/an    **today!**

(To the teacher: Encircle the hand gesture that best describes how the child worked on this activity.)

 - fairly well  - well  - very well

Teacher's Signature

QUIZ NO. 1 SCORE: ______

Write the **initial**, **medial**, or **final** sound for each picture.

 __ i __	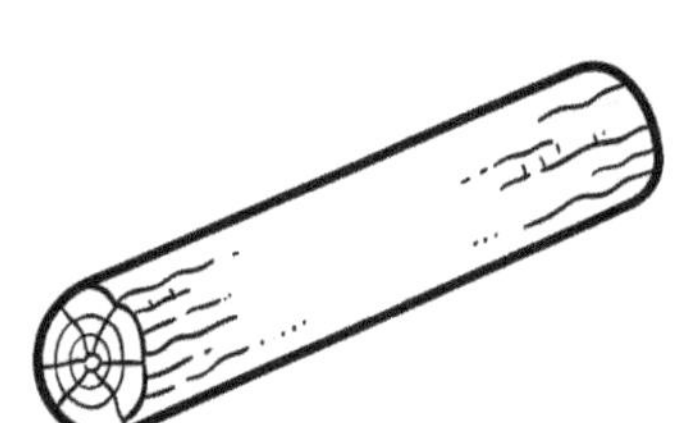 woo __
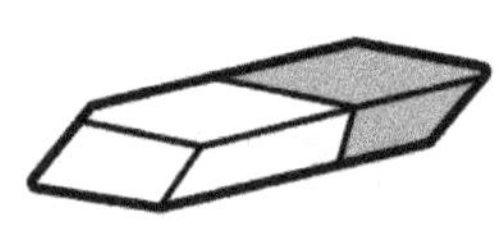 __ raser	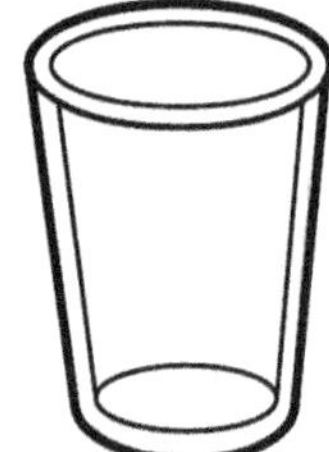 __ mpty
 __ ork	 c __ b
 pizz __	 __ racker
 __ oughnut	 __ aby

Letter **<u>Ff</u>**

This is the proper way to write the letter **<u>Ff</u>**.

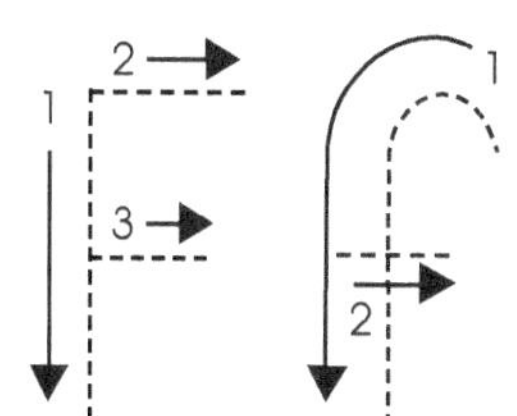

ACTIVITY 31

Practice writing the letter **<u>Ff</u>** by tracing the broken lines. Follow the direction of the arrows.

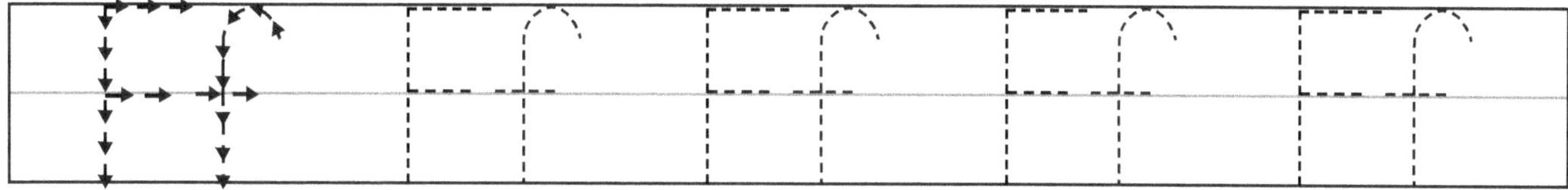

Write more letter **<u>Ff's</u>**. Make five sets. Leave equal spaces between the letter pairs.

Write the letter **<u>f</u>** where you hear its sound.

I got a/an **today!**

(To the teacher: Encircle the hand gesture that best describes how the child worked on this activity.)

 - fairly well  - well  - very well

____

Teacher's Signature

Letter Gg

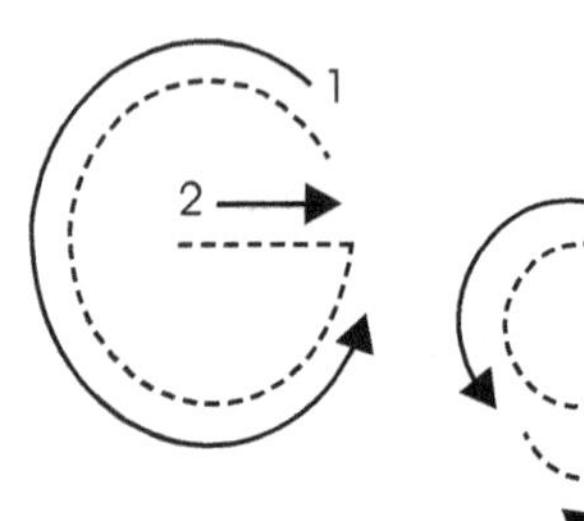

Practice writing the letter **Gg** by tracing the broken lines. Follow the direction of the arrows.

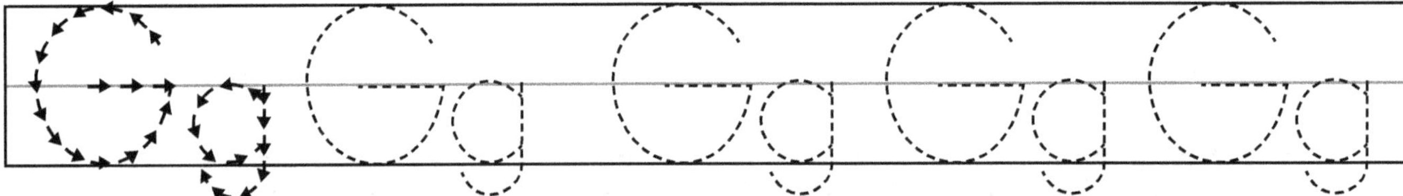

Write more letter **Gg's**. Make five sets. Leave equal spaces between the letter pairs.

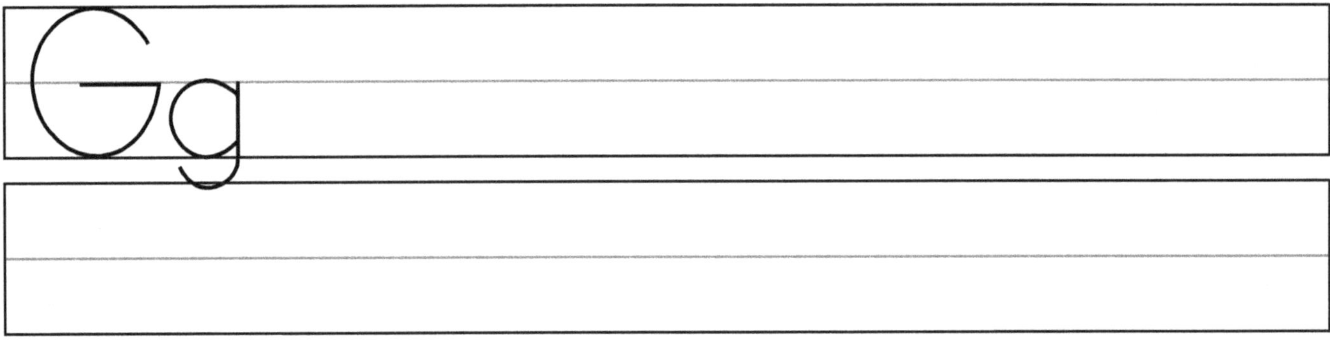

Write the letter **g** where you hear its sound.

I got a/an   **today!**

(To the teacher: Encircle the hand gesture that best describes how the child worked on this activity.)

 - fairly well  - well  - very well

____
Teacher's Signature

Letter Hh

This is the proper way to write the letter **Hh**.

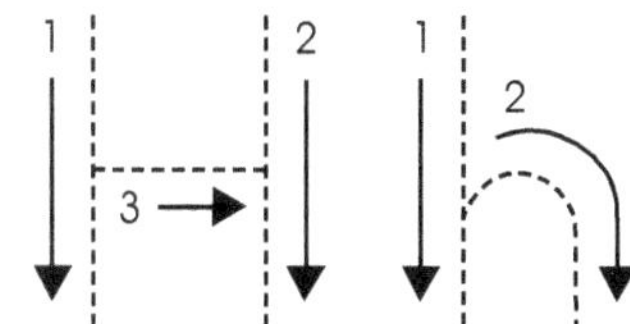

ACTIVITY 33

Practice writing the letter **Hh** by tracing the broken lines. Follow the direction of the arrows.

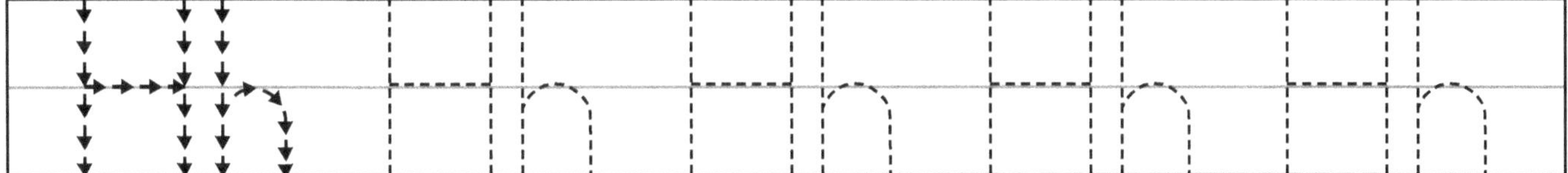

Write more letter **Hh's**. Make five sets. Leave equal spaces between the letter pairs.

Write the letter **h** where you hear its sound.

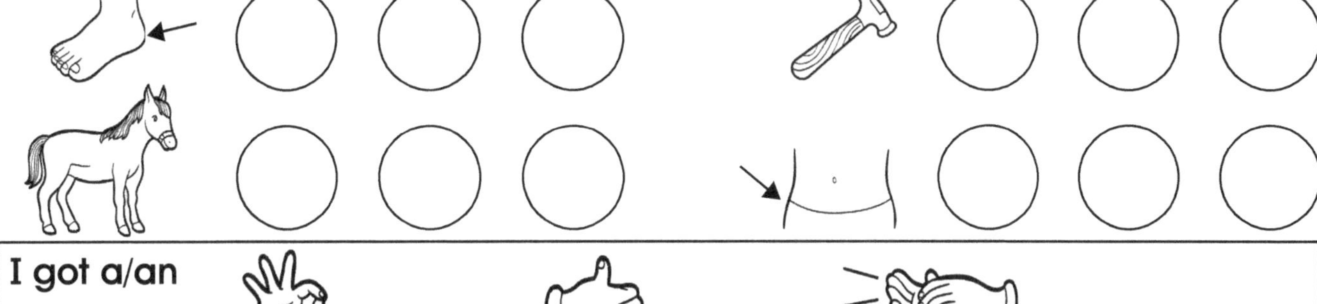

I got a/an ... today!

(To the teacher: Encircle the hand gesture that best describes how the child worked on this activity.)

 - fairly well  - well 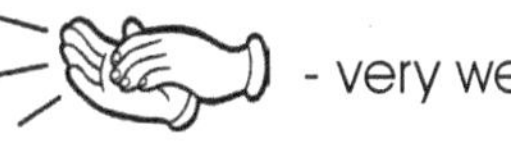 - very well

____
Teacher's Signature

Letter Ii

This is the proper way to write the letter **Ii**.

ACTIVITY 34

Practice writing the letter **Ii** by tracing the broken lines. Follow the direction of the arrows.

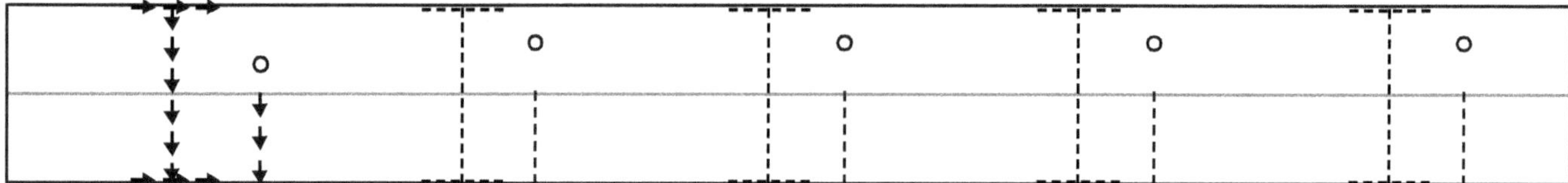

Write more letter **Ii's**. Make five sets. Leave equal spaces between the letter pairs.

Write the letter **i** where you hear its sound.

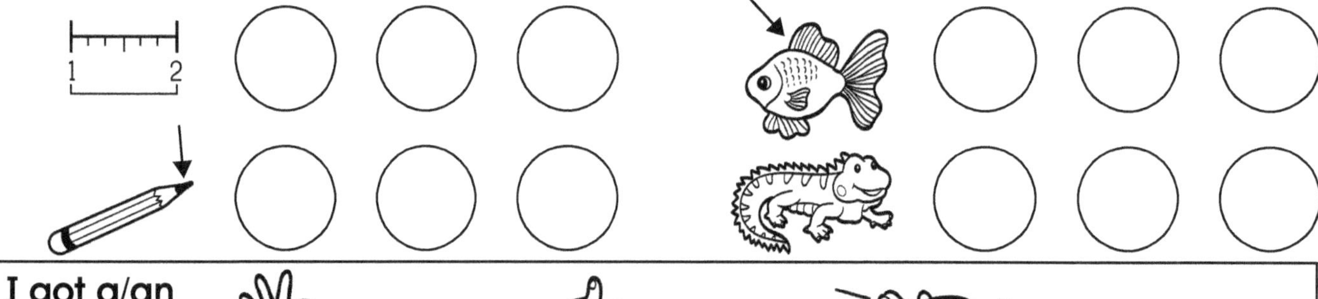

I got a/an ... **today!**

(To the teacher: Encircle the hand gesture that best describes how the child worked on this activity.)

 - fairly well  - well  - very well

Teacher's Signature

Letter Jj

This is the proper way to write the letter Jj.

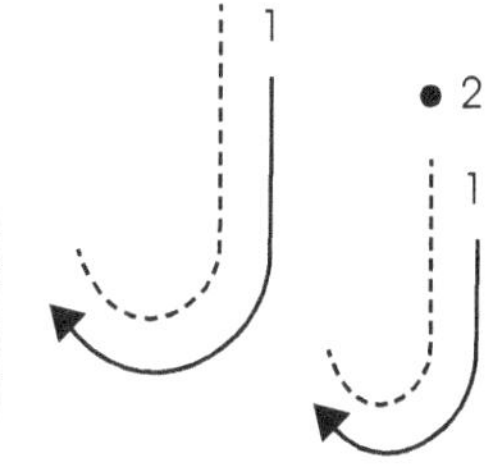

ACTIVITY 35

Practice writing the letter Jj by tracing the broken lines. Follow the direction of the arrows.

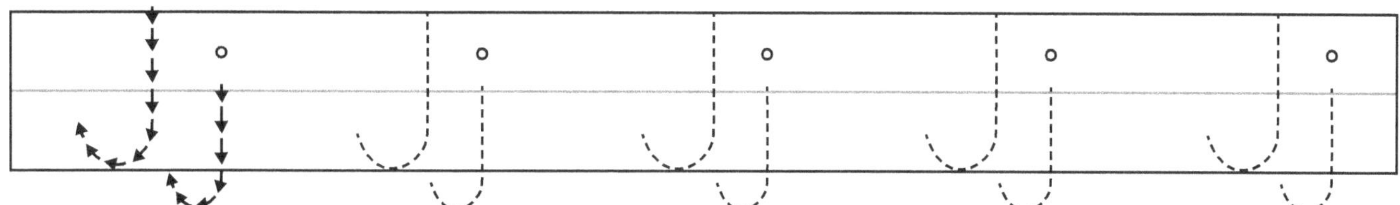

Write more letter Jj's. Make five sets. Leave equal spaces between the letter pairs.

Write the letter j where you hear its sound.

I got a/an ... today!

(To the teacher: Encircle the hand gesture that best describes how the child worked on this activity.)

 - fairly well  - well  - very well

Teacher's Signature

QUIZ NO. 2 SCORE: ______

Write the **initial**, **medial**, or **final** sound for each picture.

 __ ift	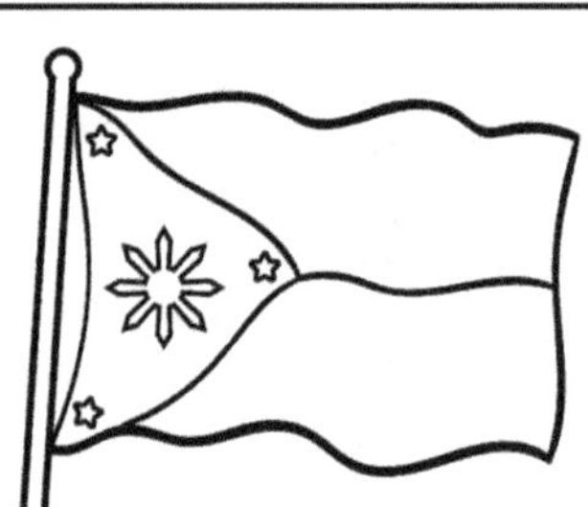 __ lag
 __ ll	 __ aguar
 wol __	 __ orn
 __ ills	 t __ ck
 __ ungle	pi __

Letter **<u>Kk</u>**

This is the proper way to write the letter **<u>Kk</u>**.

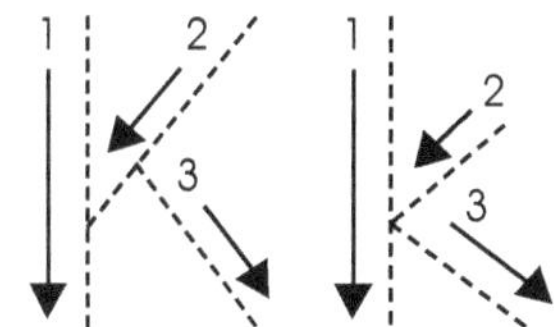

ACTIVITY 36

Practice writing the letter **<u>Kk</u>** by tracing the broken lines. Follow the direction of the arrows.

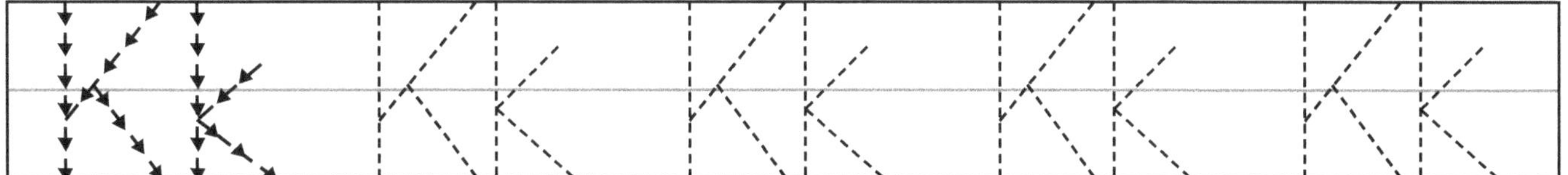

Write more letter **<u>Kk's</u>**. Make five sets. Leave equal spaces between the letter pairs.

Write the letter **<u>k</u>** where you hear its sound.

I got a/an **today!**

(To the teacher: Encircle the hand gesture that best describes how the child worked on this activity.)

 - fairly well  - well  - very well

Teacher's Signature

Letter **Ll**

This is the proper way to write the letter **Ll**.

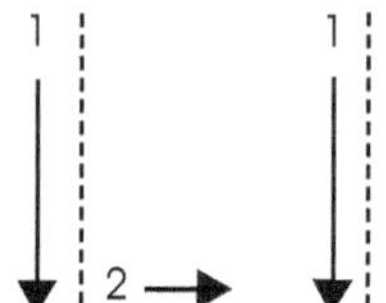

ACTIVITY 37

Practice writing the letter **Ll** by tracing the broken lines. Follow the direction of the arrows.

Write more letter **Ll's**. Make five sets. Leave equal spaces between the letter pairs.

Write the letter **l** where you hear its sound.

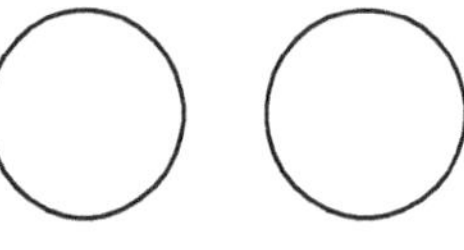

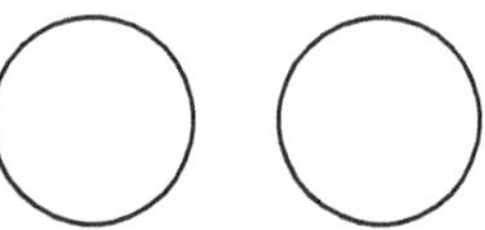
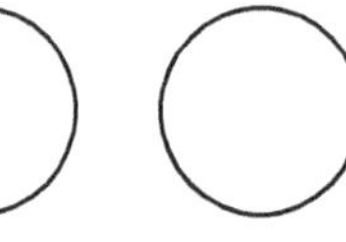

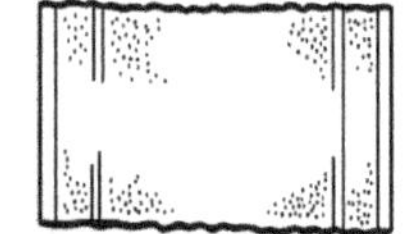
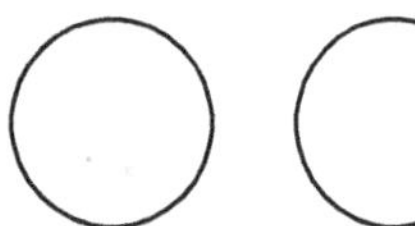
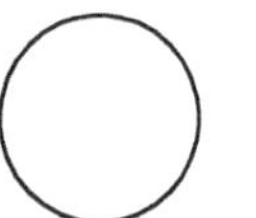

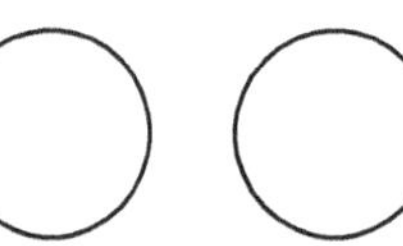

I got a/an    **today!**

(To the teacher: Encircle the hand gesture that best describes how the child worked on this activity.)

 - fairly well  - well  - very well

____
Teacher's Signature

Letter Mm

This is the proper way to write the letter **Mm**.

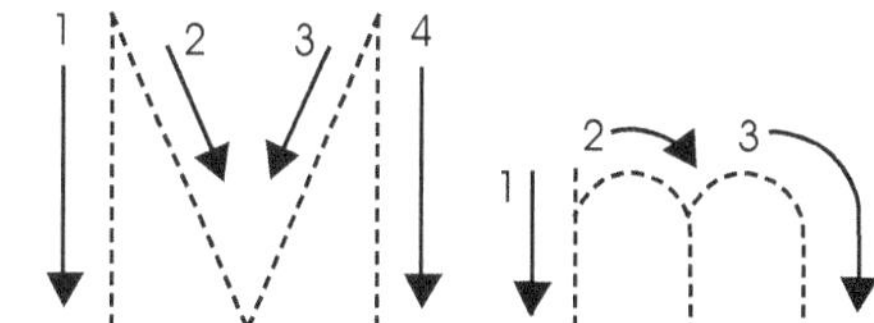

ACTIVITY 38

Practice writing the letter **Mm** by tracing the broken lines. Follow the direction of the arrows.

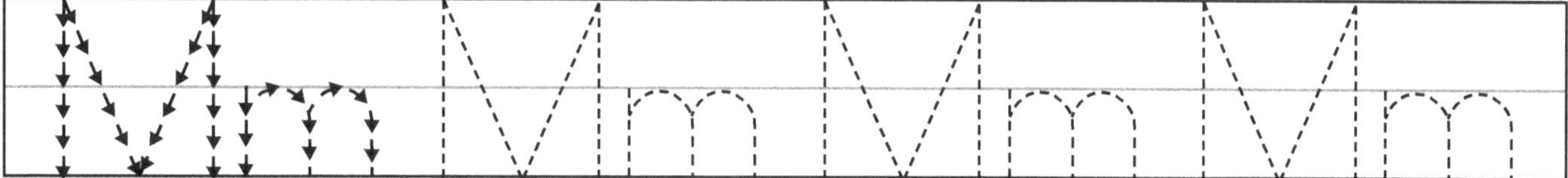

Write more letter **Mm's**. Make five sets. Leave equal spaces between the letter pairs.

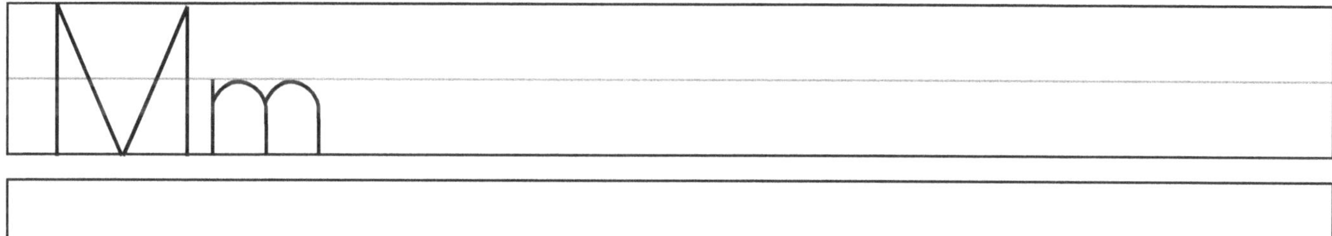

Write the letter **m** where you hear its sound.

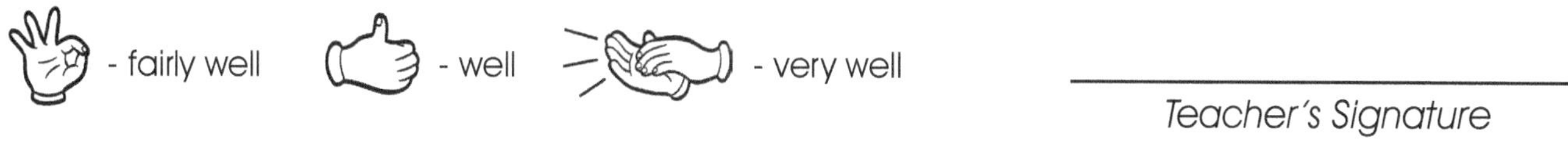

(To the teacher: Encircle the hand gesture that best describes how the child worked on this activity.)

- fairly well - well - very well

Teacher's Signature

Letter **Nn**

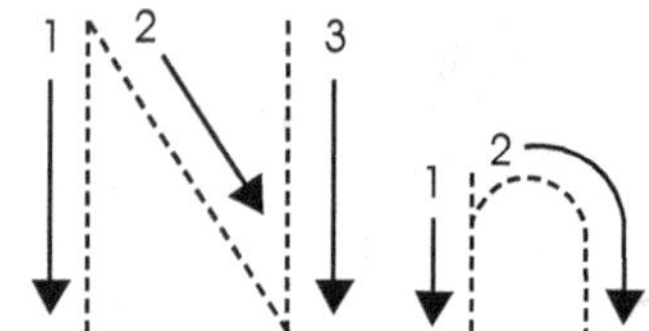

Practice writing the letter **Nn** by tracing the broken lines. Follow the direction of the arrows.

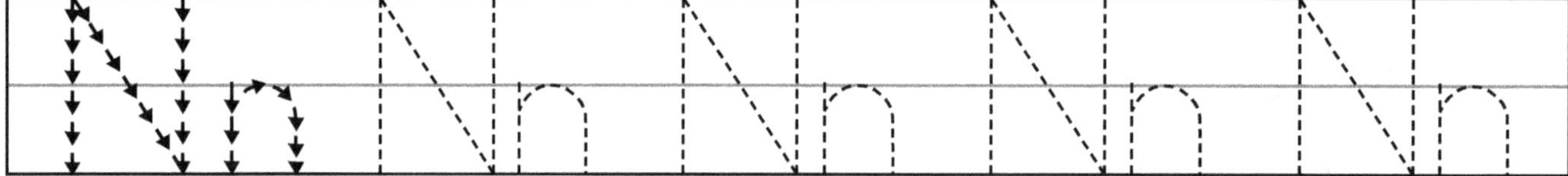

Write more letter **Nn's**. Make five sets. Leave equal spaces between the letter pairs.

Write the letter **n** where you hear its sound.

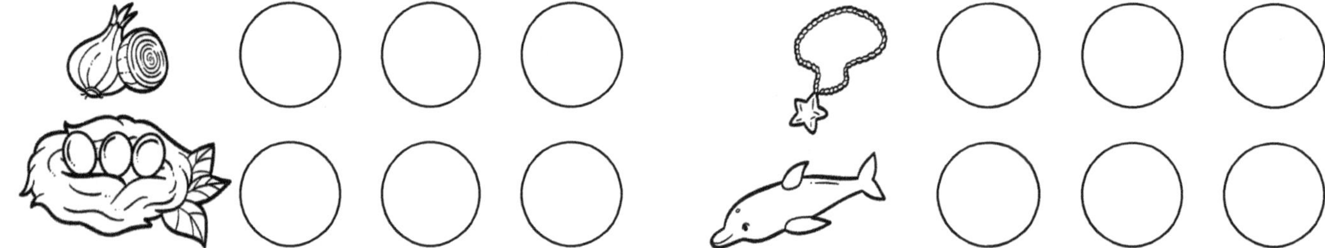

I got a/an    today!

(To the teacher: Encircle the hand gesture that best describes how the child worked on this activity.)

 - fairly well  - well  - very well

____
Teacher's Signature

Letter Oo

This is the proper way to write the letter **Oo**.

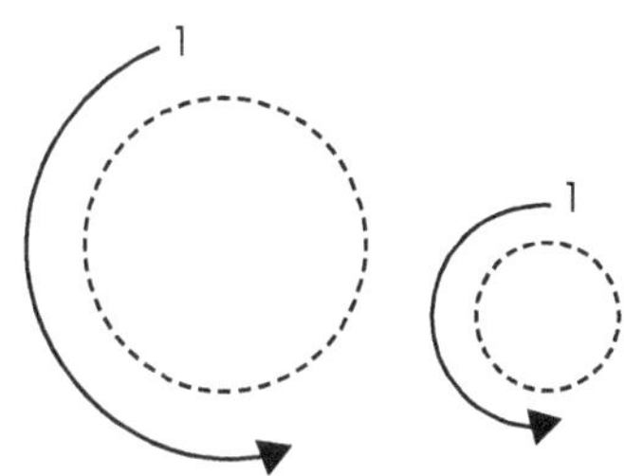

Practice writing the letter **Oo** by tracing the broken lines. Follow the direction of the arrows.

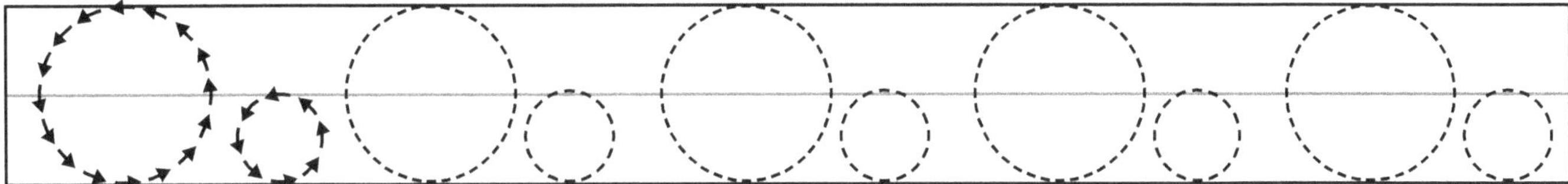

Write more letter **Oo's**. Make five sets. Leave equal spaces between the letter pairs.

Write the letter **o** where you hear its sound.

I got a/an ... today!

(To the teacher: Encircle the hand gesture that best describes how the child worked on this activity.)

 - fairly well  - well  - very well

____
Teacher's Signature

QUIZ NO. 3 SCORE: ______

Write the **initial**, **medial**, or **final** sound for each picture.

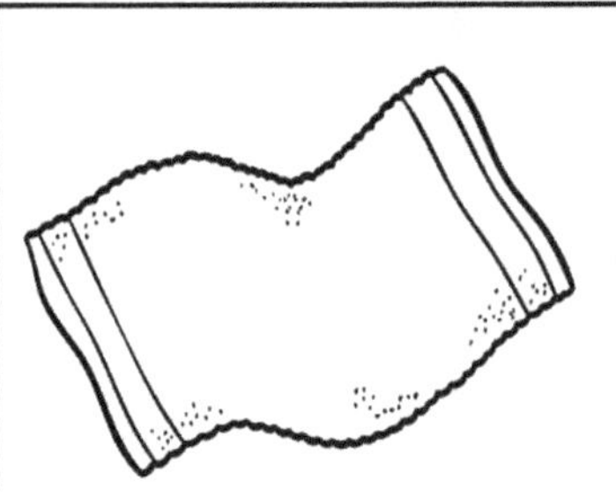 towe __	 __ angaroo
 l __ ck	 broo __
 hoo __	 spoo __
 __ eedle	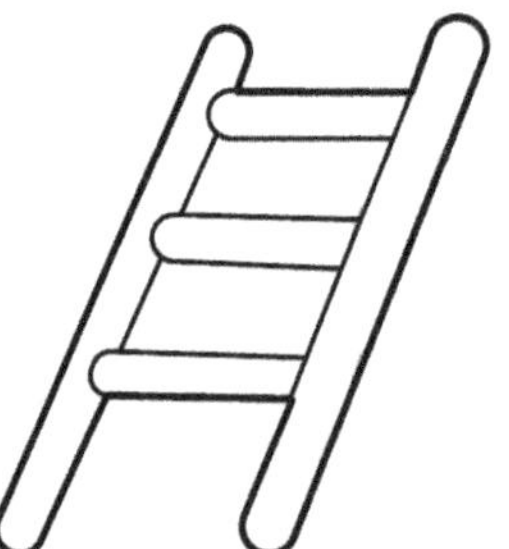 __ adder
 __ agnet	 __ stritch

Letter Pp

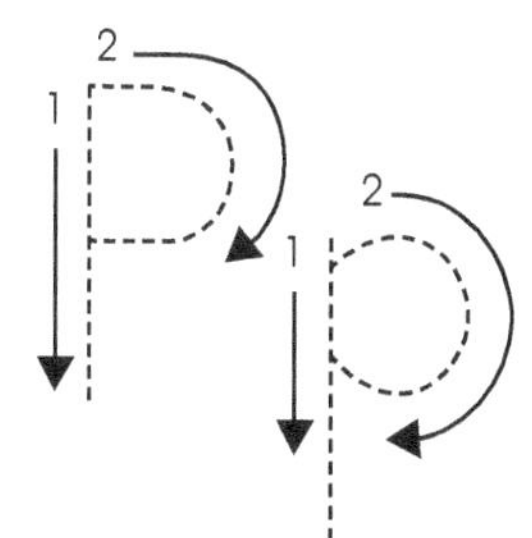

ACTIVITY 41

Practice writing the letter **Pp** by tracing the broken lines. Follow the direction of the arrows.

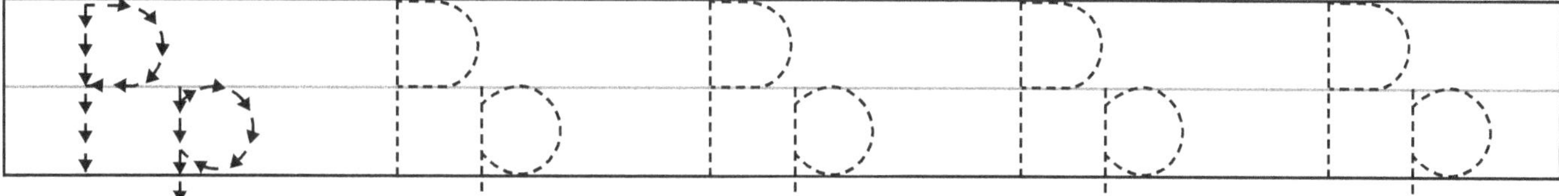

Write more letter **Pp's**. Make five sets. Leave equal spaces between the letter pairs.

Write the letter **p** where you hear its sound.

I got a/an ... **today!**

(To the teacher: Encircle the hand gesture that best describes how the child worked on this activity.)

 - fairly well  - well  - very well

____
Teacher's Signature

Letter Qq

This is the proper way to write the letter **Qq**.

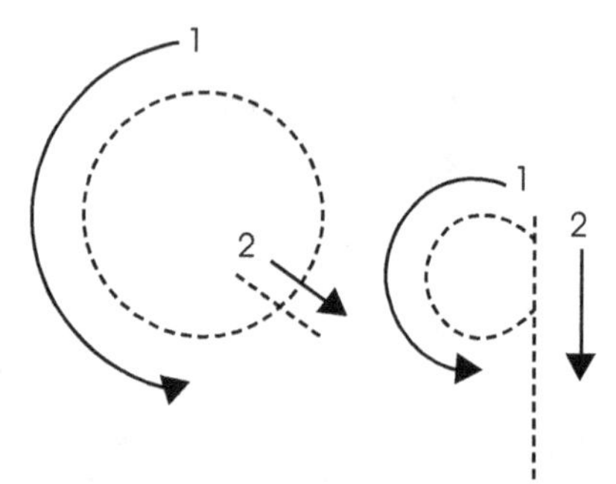

ACTIVITY 42

Practice writing the letter **Qq** by tracing the broken lines. Follow the direction of the arrows.

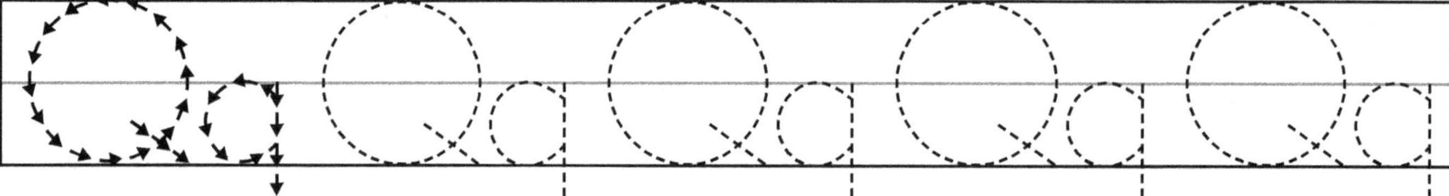

Write more letter **Qq's**. Make five sets. Leave equal spaces between the letter pairs.

Write the letter **q** where you hear its sound.

I got a/an   **today!**

(To the teacher: Encircle the hand gesture that best describes how the child worked on this activity.)

 - fairly well  - well 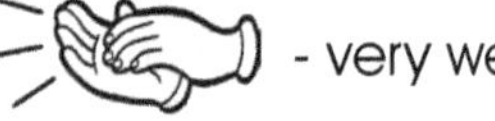 - very well

____

Teacher's Signature

Letter Rr

This is the proper way to write the letter **Rr**.

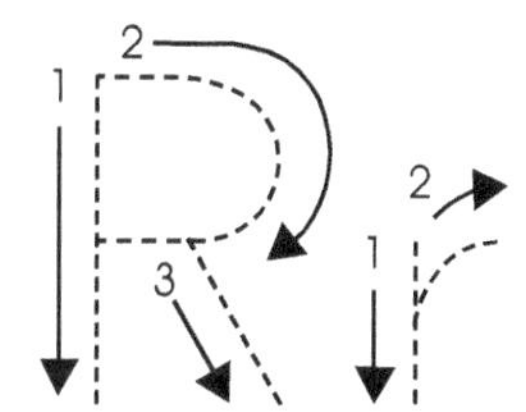

ACTIVITY 43

Practice writing the letter **Rr** by tracing the broken lines. Follow the direction of the arrows.

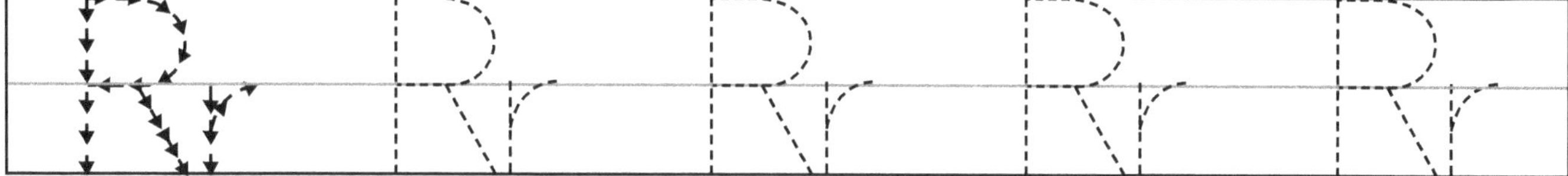

Write more letter **Rr's**. Make five sets. Leave equal spaces between the letter pairs.

Write the letter **r** where you hear its sound.

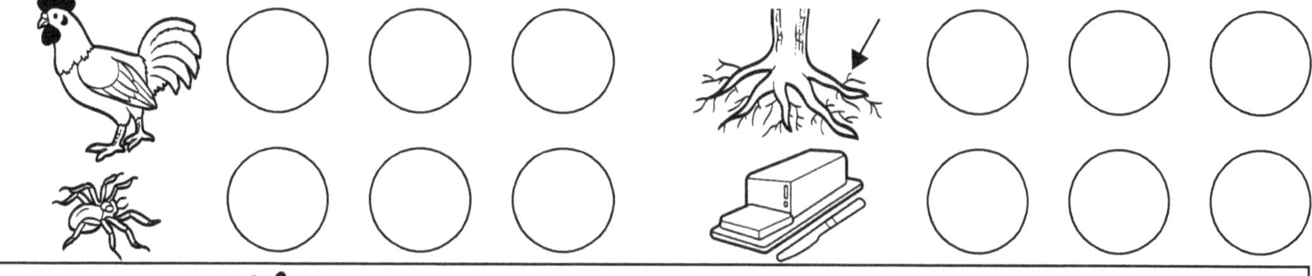

I got a/an    **today!**

(To the teacher: Encircle the hand gesture that best describes how the child worked on this activity.)

 - fairly well  - well  - very well

____

Teacher's Signature

Letter Ss

This is the proper way to write the letter **Ss**.

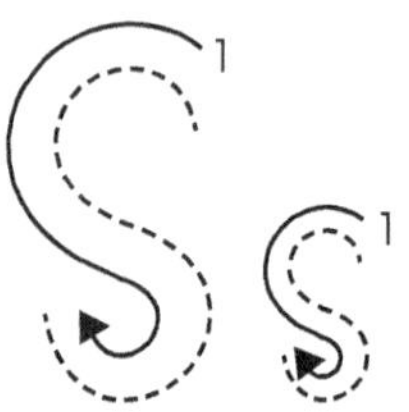

ACTIVITY 44

Practice writing the letter **Ss** by tracing the broken lines. Follow the direction of the arrows.

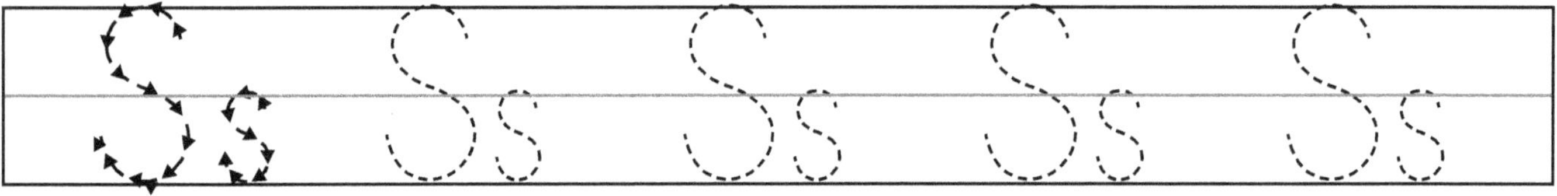

Write more letter **Ss's**. Make five sets. Leave equal spaces between the letter pairs.

Ss

Write the letter **s** where you hear its sound.

I got a/an   **today!**

(To the teacher: Encircle the hand gesture that best describes how the child worked on this activity.)

 - fairly well  - well  - very well

Teacher's Signature

Letter **<u>Tt</u>**

This is the proper way to write the letter **<u>Tt</u>**.

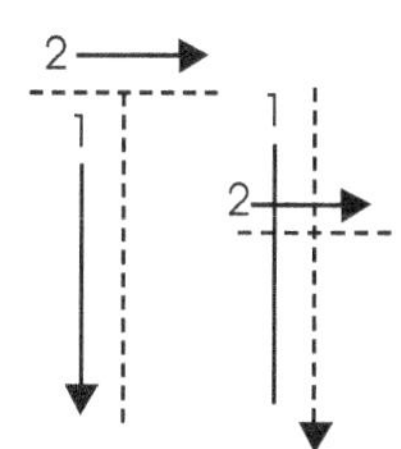

ACTIVITY 45

Practice writing the letter **<u>Tt</u>** by tracing the broken lines. Follow the direction of the arrows.

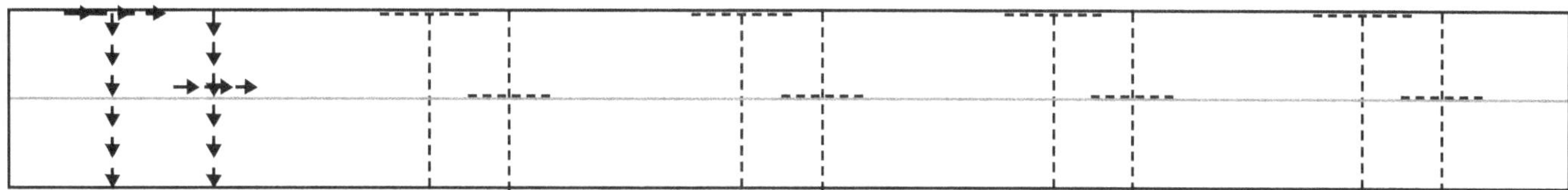

Write more letter **<u>Tt's</u>**. Make five sets. Leave equal spaces between the letter pairs.

Write the letter **<u>t</u>** where you hear its sound.

(To the teacher: Encircle the hand gesture that best describes how the child worked on this activity.)

 - fairly well  - well  - very well

Teacher's Signature

QUIZ NO. 4 SCORE: ______

Write the **initial**, **medial**, or **final** sound for each picture.

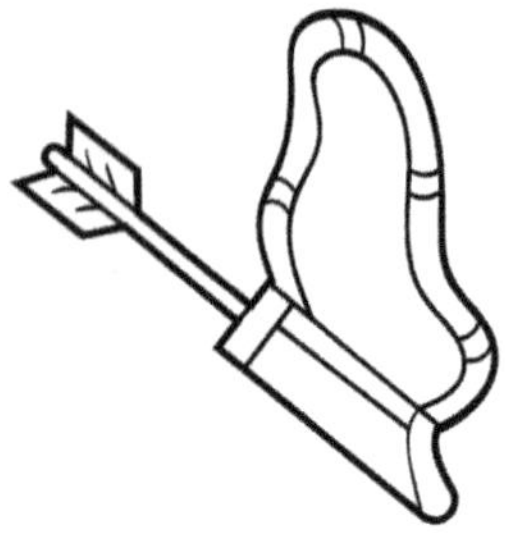

__ uiver	shi__
hange__	__ailor
pocke__	__en__
__ants	__iger
lotu __	__ive__

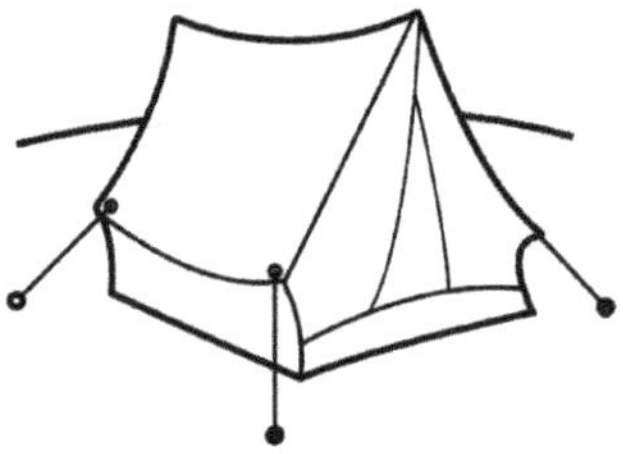

Letter Uu

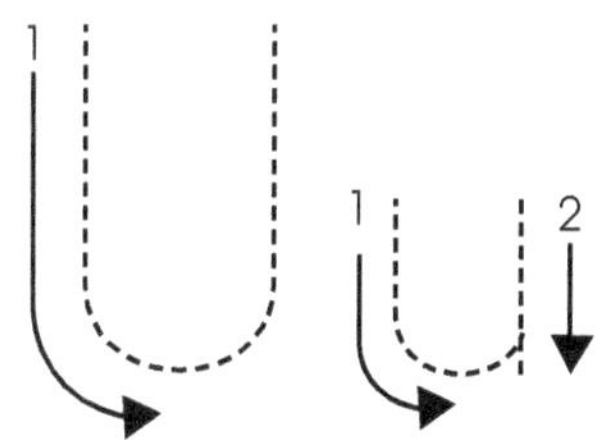

ACTIVITY 46

Practice writing the letter **Uu** by tracing the broken lines. Follow the direction of the arrows.

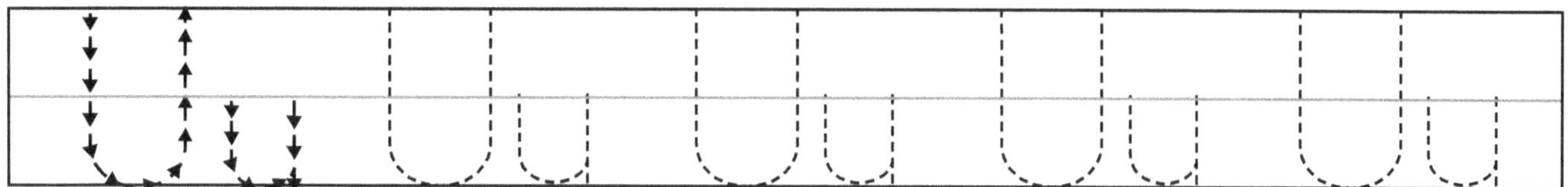

Write more letter **Uu's**. Make five sets. Leave equal spaces between the letter pairs.

Write the letter **u** where you hear its sound.

I got a/an    **today!**

(To the teacher: Encircle the hand gesture that best describes how the child worked on this activity.)

 - fairly well  - well  - very well

____
Teacher's Signature

Letter Vv

This is the proper way to write the letter **Vv**.

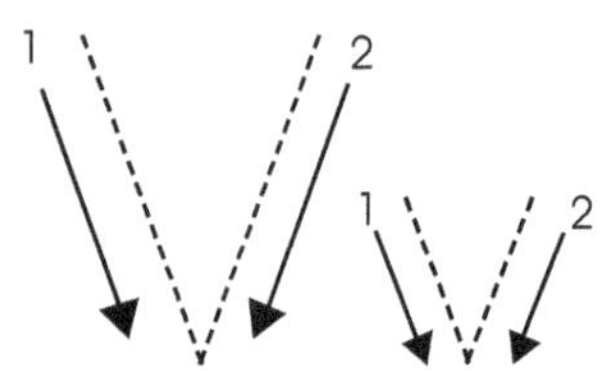

Practice writing the letter **Vv** by tracing the broken lines. Follow the direction of the arrows.

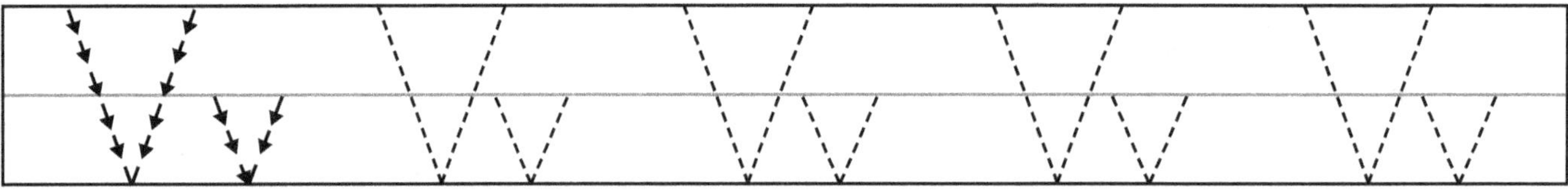

Write more letter **Vv's**. Make five sets. Leave equal spaces between the letter pairs.

Write the letter **v** where you hear its sound.

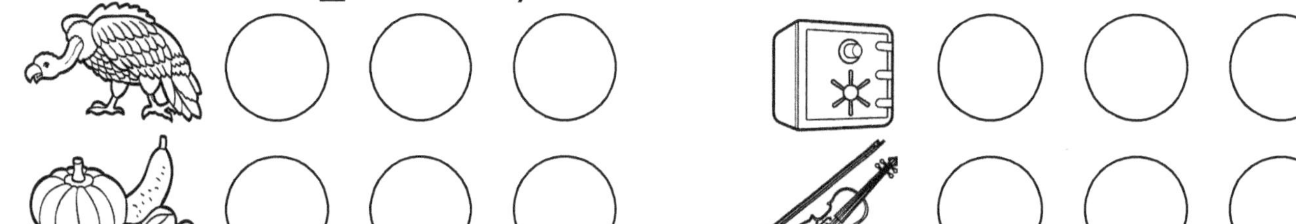

I got a/an   today!

(To the teacher: Encircle the hand gesture that best describes how the child worked on this activity.)

 - fairly well  - well - very well

Teacher's Signature

Letter Ww

This is the proper way to write the letter **Ww**.

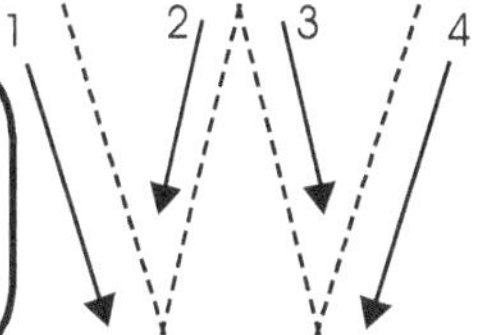

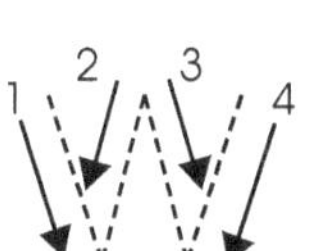

ACTIVITY 48

Practice writing the letter **Ww** by tracing the broken lines. Follow the direction of the arrows.

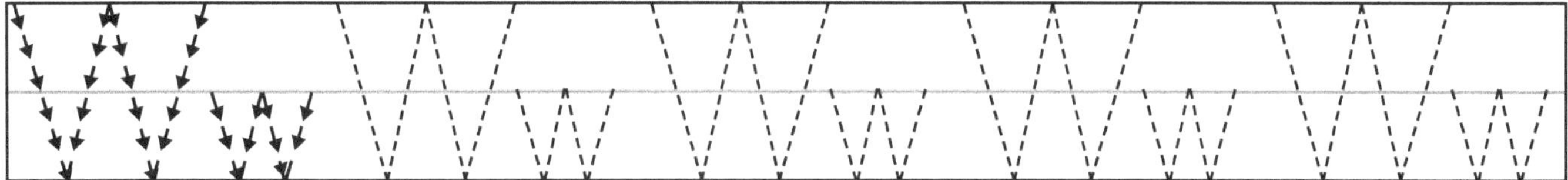

Write more letter **Ww's**. Make five sets. Leave equal spaces between the letter pairs.

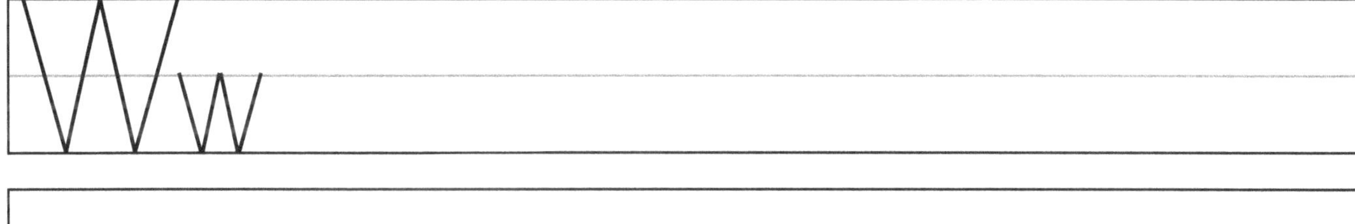

Write the letter **w** where you hear its sound.

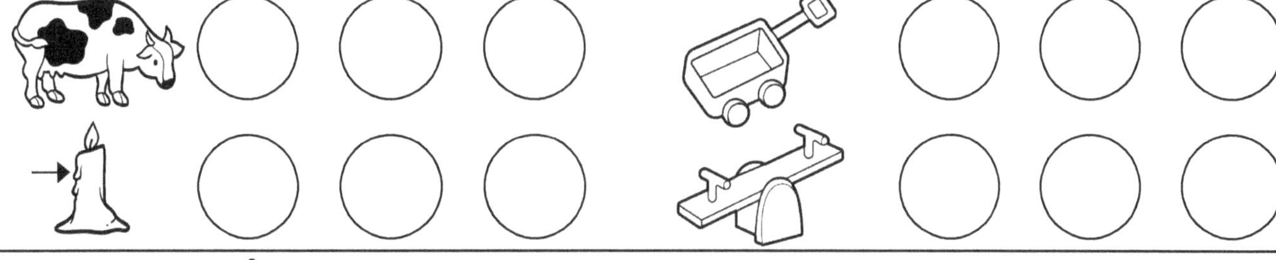

I got a/an    **today!**

(To the teacher: Encircle the hand gesture that best describes how the child worked on this activity.)

 - fairly well  - well - very well

Teacher's Signature

Letter Xx

This is the proper way to write the letter **Xx**.

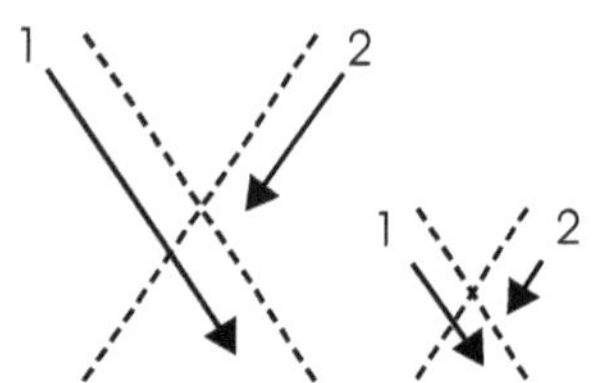

ACTIVITY 49

Practice writing the letter **Xx** by tracing the broken lines. Follow the direction of the arrows.

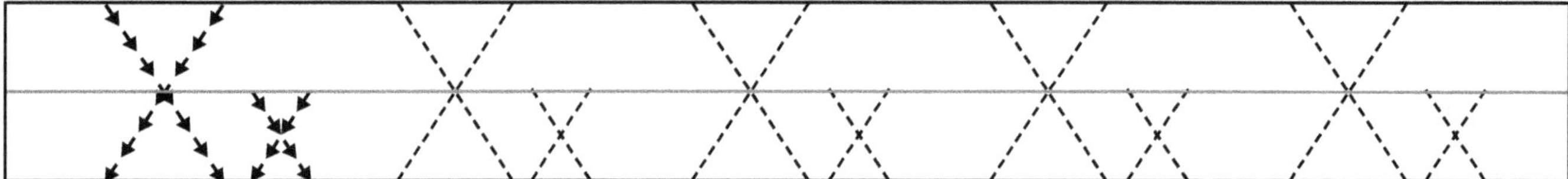

Write more letter **Xx's**. Make five sets. Leave equal spaces between the letter pairs.

Write the letter **x** where you hear its sound.

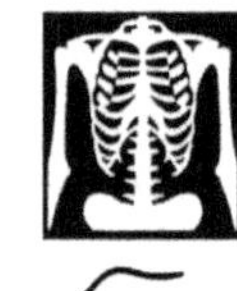
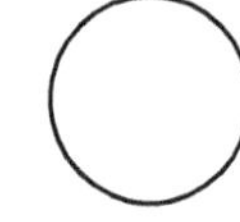

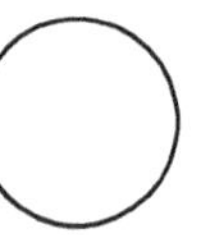

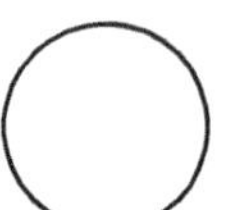

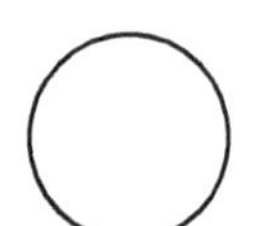
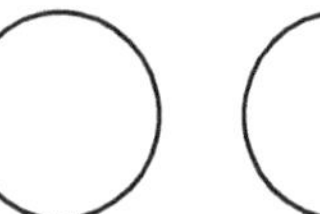

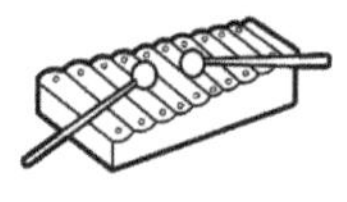
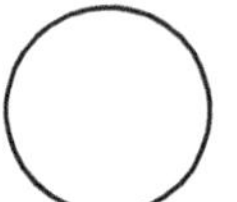

I got a/an    **today!**

(To the teacher: Encircle the hand gesture that best describes how the child worked on this activity.)

 - fairly well  - well  - very well

____

Teacher's Signature

Letter Yy

This is the proper way to write the letter **Yy**.

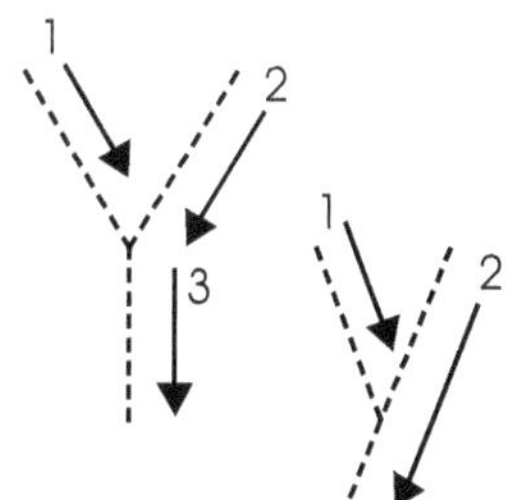

ACTIVITY 50

Practice writing the letter **Yy** by tracing the broken lines. Follow the direction of the arrows.

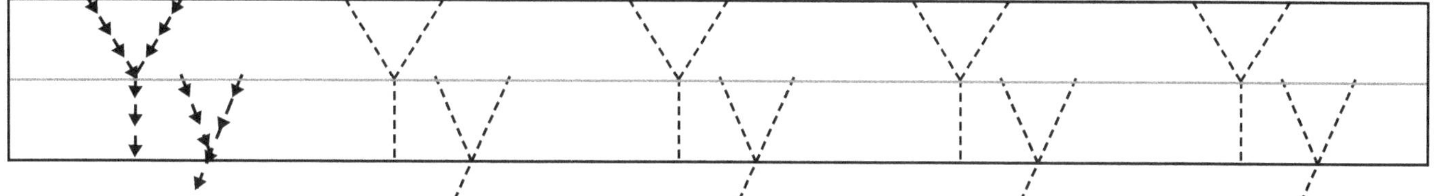

Write more letter **Yy's**. Make five sets. Leave equal spaces between the letter pairs.

Write the letter **y** where you hear its sound.

I got a/an    **today!**

(To the teacher: Encircle the hand gesture that best describes how the child worked on this activity.)

 - fairly well  - well  - very well

____
Teacher's Signature

Letter Zz

This is the proper way to write the letter **Zz**.

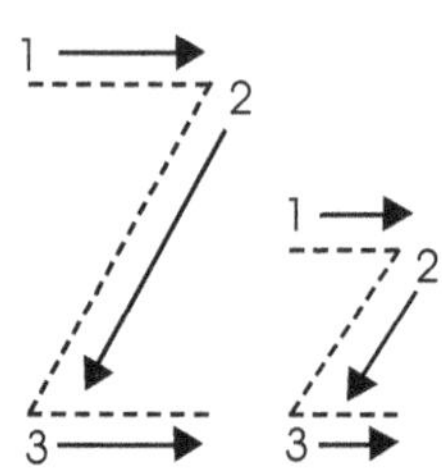

ACTIVITY 51

Practice writing the letter **Zz** by tracing the broken lines. Follow the direction of the arrows.

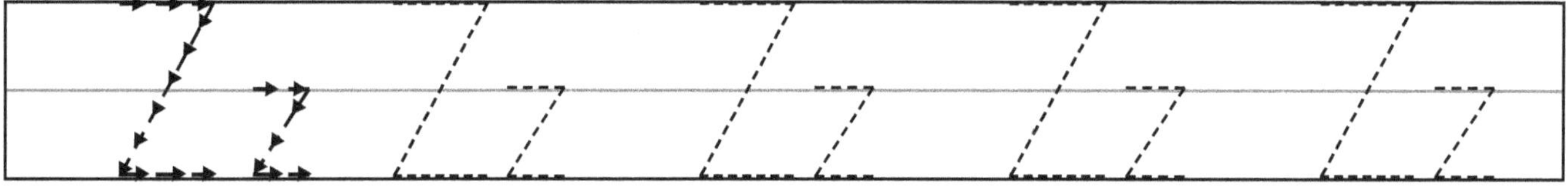

Write more letter **Zz's**. Make five sets. Leave equal spaces between the letter pairs.

Write the letter **z** where you hear its sound.

I got a/an   **today!**

(To the teacher: Encircle the hand gesture that best describes how the child worked on this activity.)

 - fairly well  - well  - very well

Teacher's Signature

QUIZ NO. 5 SCORE: ______

Write the **initial**, **medial**, or **final** sound for each picture.

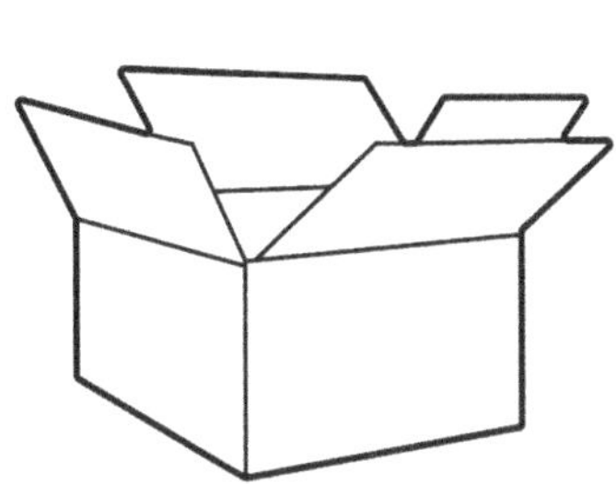

bo __

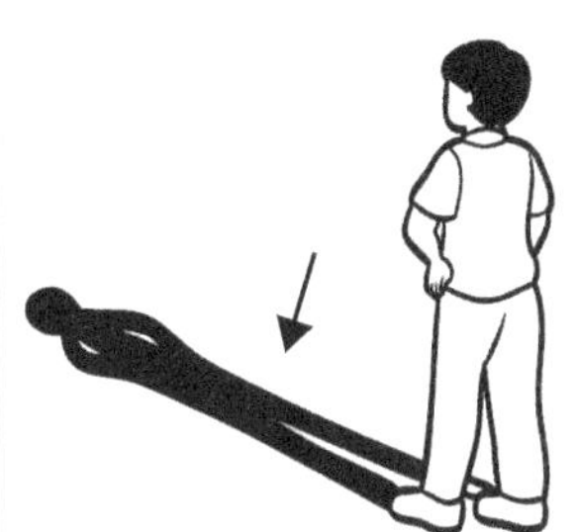

shado __

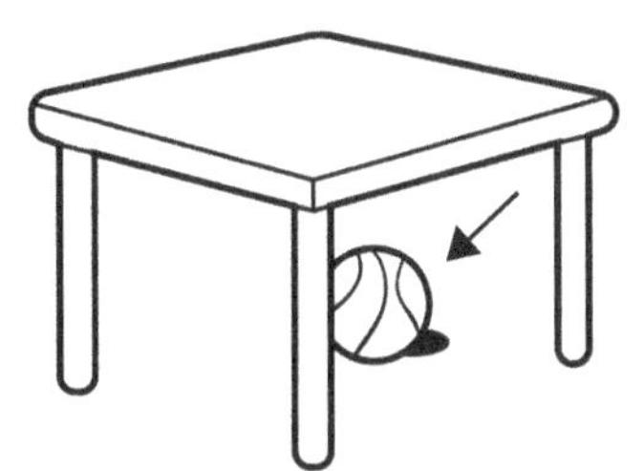

__ nder

pla __

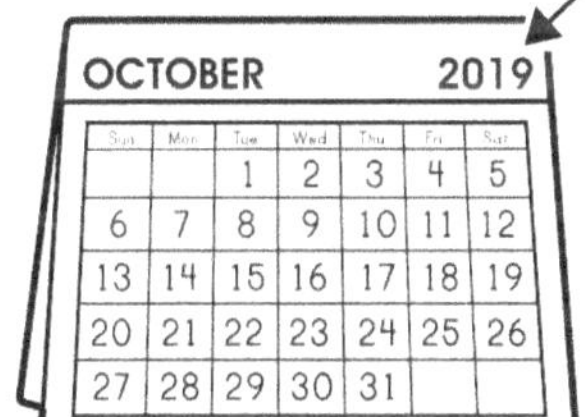

__ ear

b __ n

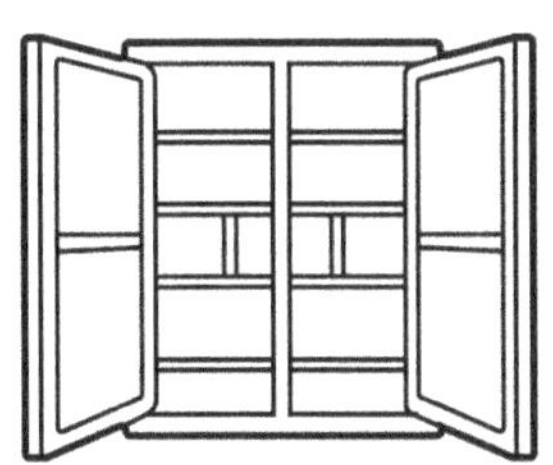

__ indo __

__ ine

__ ebra

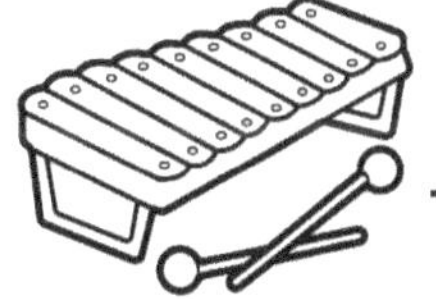

__ ylophone

Write the uppercase and the lowercase letters of the alphabet in their correct order. Follow the proper strokes in writing letters, leaving equal spaces between the letter pairs.

I got a/an today!

(To the teacher: Encircle the hand gesture that best describes how the child worked on this activity.)

- fairly well - well - very well

Teacher's Signature

PROGRESS CHART
FIRST QUARTER

NAME: ______________________________ LEVEL: ______________

Activity	What I Got			Quiz	No. of Items	My Score
1				1	10	
2				2	10	
3				3	10	
4				4	10	
5				5	10	
6						
7						
8						
9						
10						
11						
12						
13						
14						
15						
16						
17						
18						
19						
20						
21						
22						
23						
24						
25						
26						

Activity	What I Got			Quiz	No. of Items	My Score
27						
28						
29						
30						
31						
32						
33						
34						
35						
36						
37						
38						
39						
40						
41						
42						
43						
44						
45						
46						
47						
48						
49						
50						
51						
52				TOTAL	50	

____
Parent's/Guardian's Signature

____
Teacher's Signature

Legend:  fairly well  well  very well

SECOND QUARTER

Teacher's Objectives and Student Evaluation

Lesson	*At the end of the activities, the child should be able to:*			
1	1. write the numerals and number words one to ten with proper strokes			
	2. copy the numerals and number words one to ten with correct spacing			
2	3. copy names of animals on lined paper			
	4. be familiarized with rare animals			
	5. use uniform spacing between letters			
3	6. copy names of colors correctly, putting emphasis on proper spacing between words			
	7. master the different colors			
4	8. copy names of family members, putting emphasis on proper spacing between words			
	9. get acquainted with other family members			
5	10. write the days of the week on lined paper			
	11. master writing words with uppercase and lowercase letters			
6	12. write the months of the year on lined paper			
	13. reproduce words with uppercase and lowercase letters			
7	14. write action words on lined paper			
	15. read and understand the meaning of some action words			
	16. use uniform spacing between action words			
8	17. write describing words on lined paper			
	18. read and master the meaning of some describing words			
	19. use uniform spacing between describing words			

Legend:  fairly well  well  very well

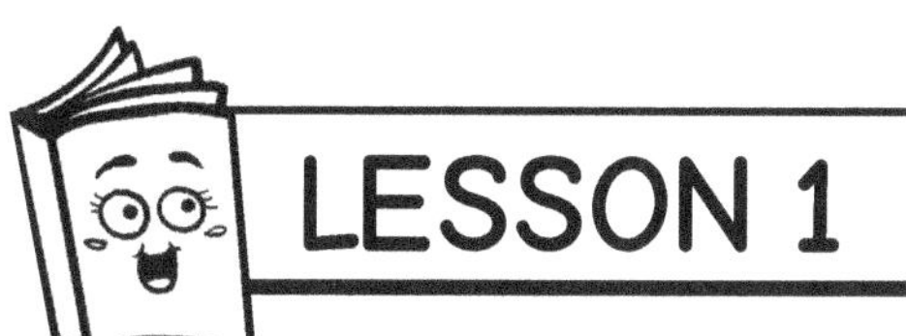

LESSON 1

THE NUMERALS AND NUMBER WORDS

1 – one

This is the proper way to write the numeral **1**.

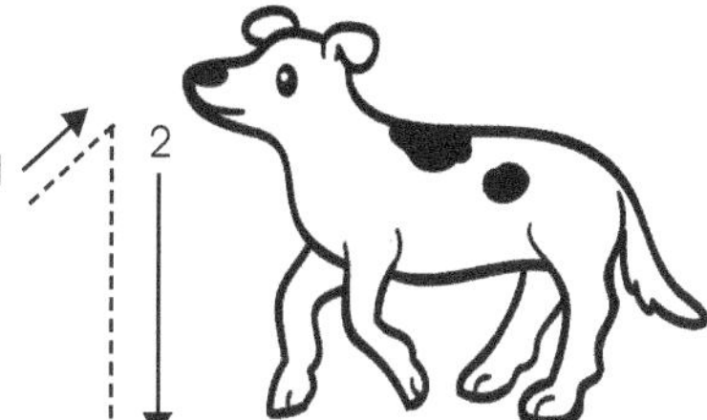

ACTIVITY 1

Practice writing the numeral **1** by tracing the broken lines. Follow the direction of the arrows.

Write more numeral **1's**. Make five sets. Leave equal spaces between the numerals.

1

Write the number word **one**. Make three sets in each row.

one

I got a/an    **today!**

(To the teacher: Encircle the hand gesture that best describes how the child worked on this activity.)

 - fairly well  - well  - very well

____
Teacher's Signature

Count the objects and then write the correct numeral and number word.

Numeral	Number Word
 1	one

I got a/an (fairly well) (well) (very well) today!

(To the teacher: Encircle the hand gesture that best describes how the child worked on this activity.)

- fairly well  - well  - very well

Teacher's Signature

2 – two

This is the proper way to write the numeral **2**.

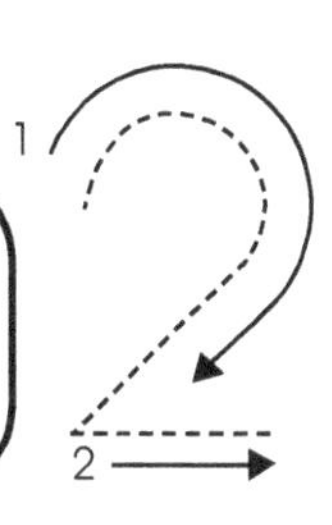

ACTIVITY 3

Practice writing the numeral **2** by tracing the broken lines. Follow the direction of the arrows.

Write more numeral **2's**. Make five sets. Leave equal spaces between the numerals.

2

Write the number word **two**. Make three sets in each row.

two

I got a/an    **today!**

(To the teacher: Encircle the hand gesture that best describes how the child worked on this activity.)

 - fairly well  - well  - very well

____
Teacher's Signature

ACTIVITY 4

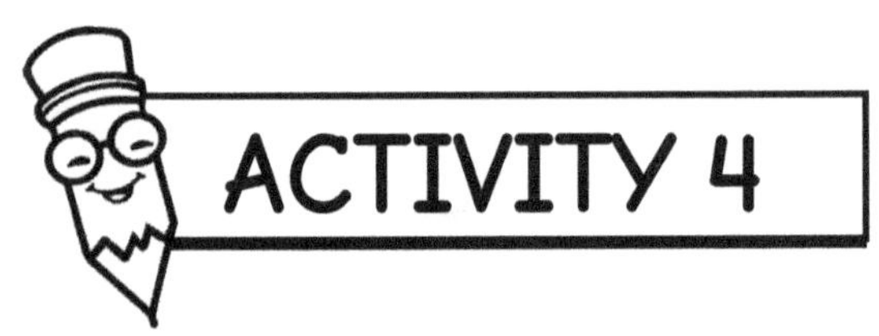

Count the objects and then write the correct numeral and number word.

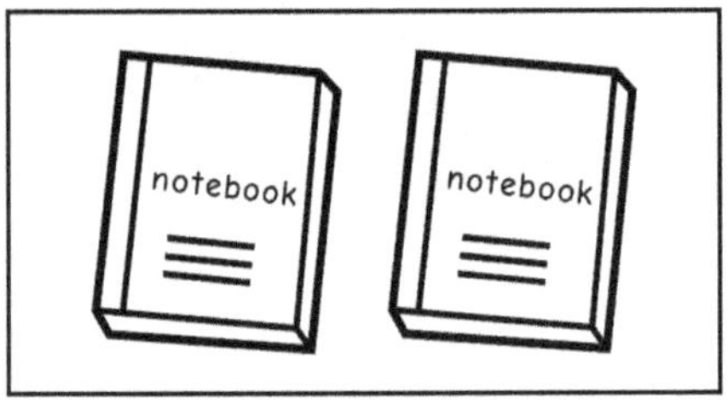

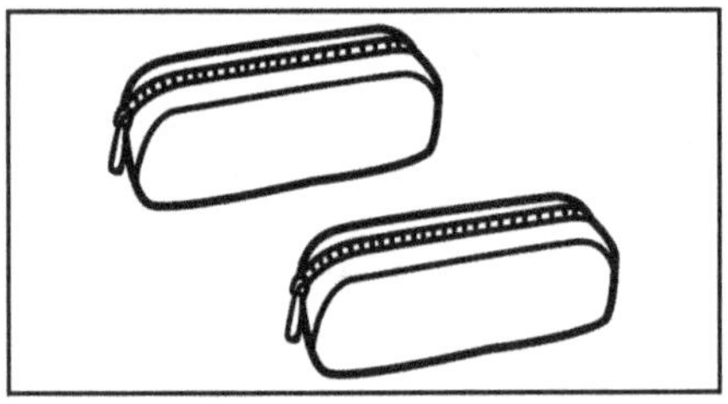

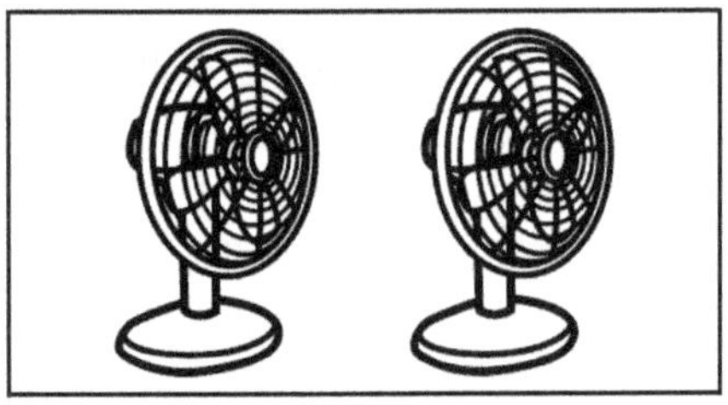

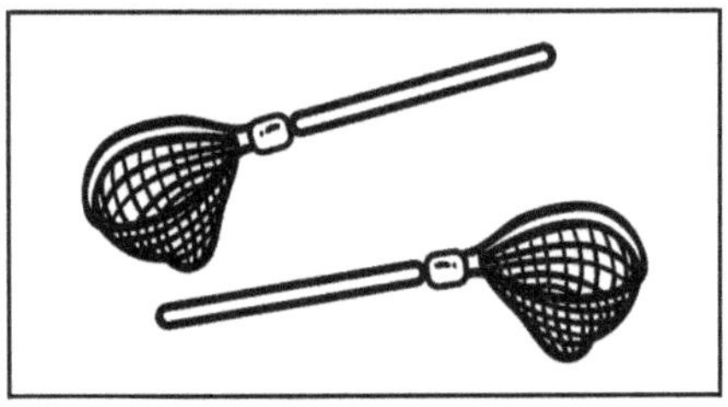

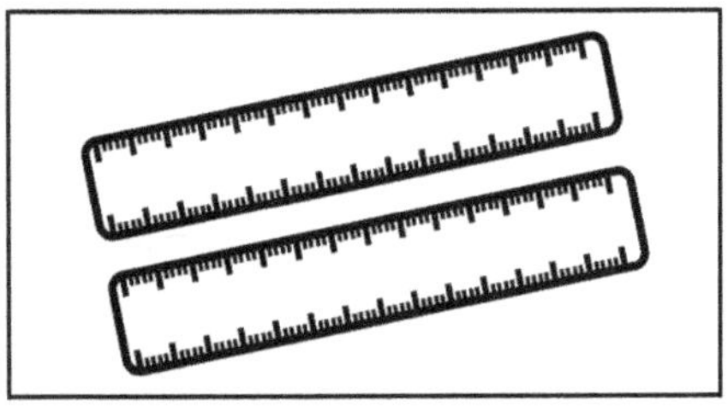

Numeral	Number Word
2	two

I got a/an 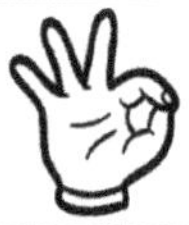 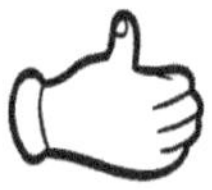 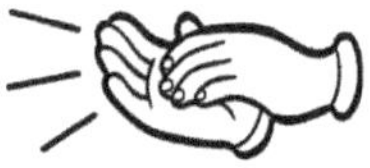 **today!**

(To the teacher: Encircle the hand gesture that best describes how the child worked on this activity.)

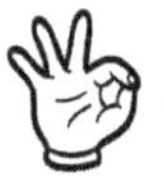 - fairly well 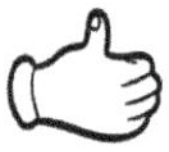 - well 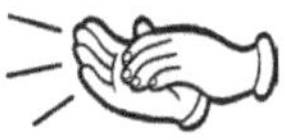 - very well

____
Teacher's Signature

3 – three

This is the proper way to write the numeral **3**.

ACTIVITY 5

Practice writing the numeral **3** by tracing the broken lines. Follow the direction of the arrows.

3 3 3 3 3

Write more numeral **3's**. Make five sets. Leave equal spaces between the numerals.

3

Write the number word **three**. Make three sets in each row.

three

I got a/an    today!

(To the teacher: Encircle the hand gesture that best describes how the child worked on this activity.)

 - fairly well  - well - very well

Teacher's Signature

ACTIVITY 6

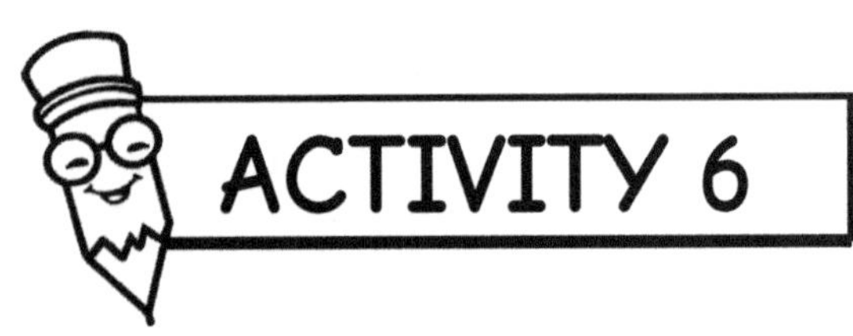

Count the objects and then write the correct numeral and number word.

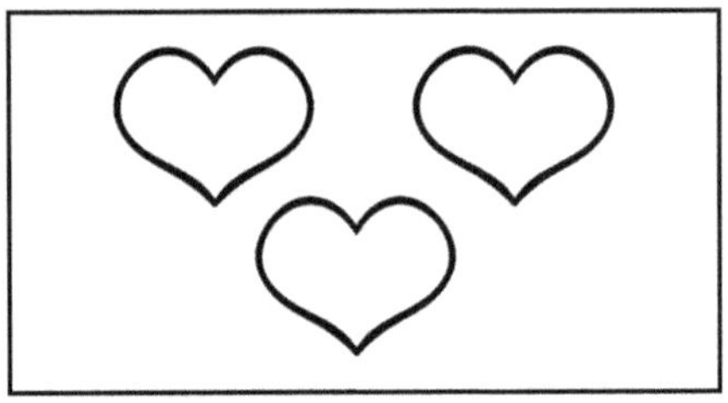

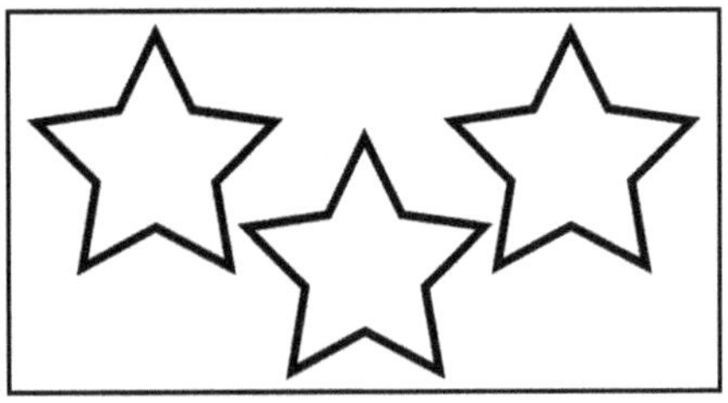

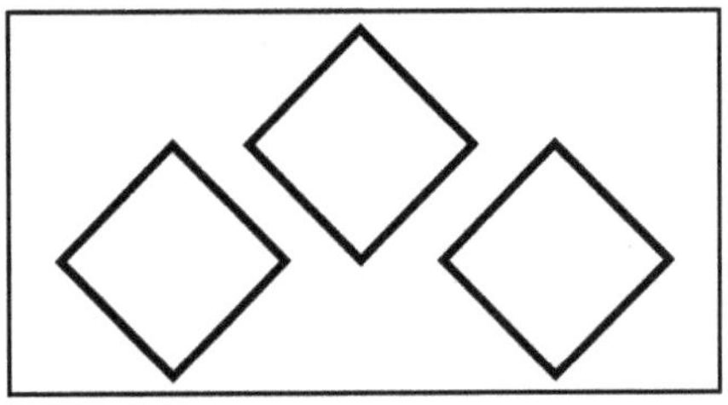

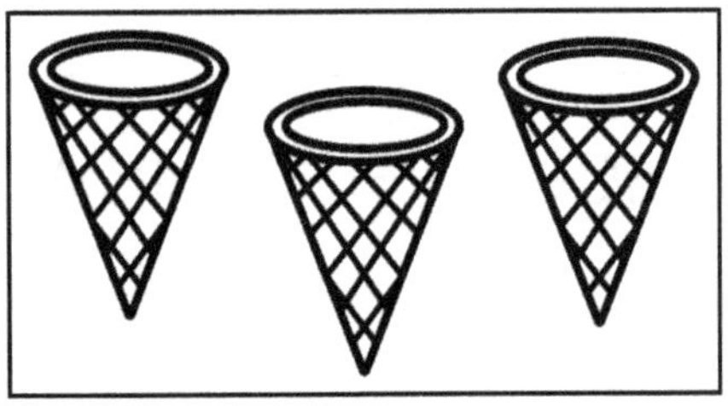

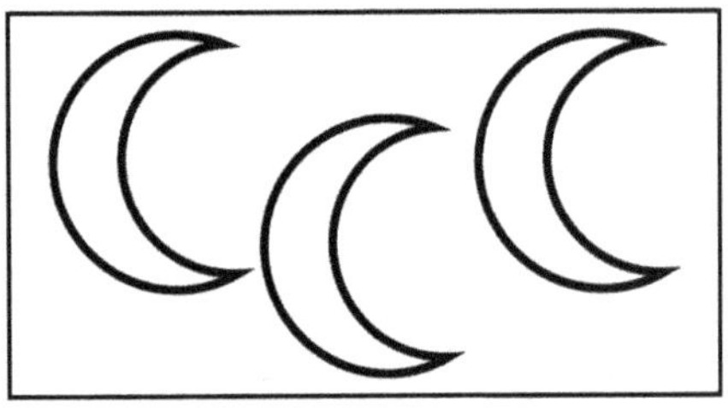

Numeral	Number Word
3	three

I got a/an 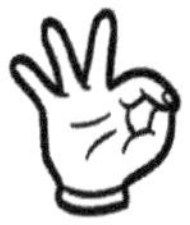 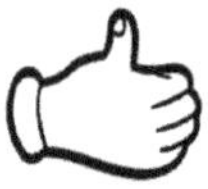 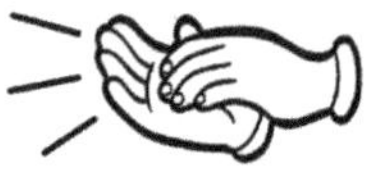 **today!**

(To the teacher: Encircle the hand gesture that best describes how the child worked on this activity.)

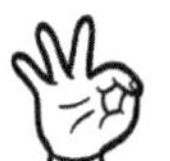

 - fairly well - well - very well

____

Teacher's Signature

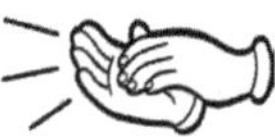

QUIZ NO. 1 SCORE: ______

Count the objects and then write the correct numeral and number word.

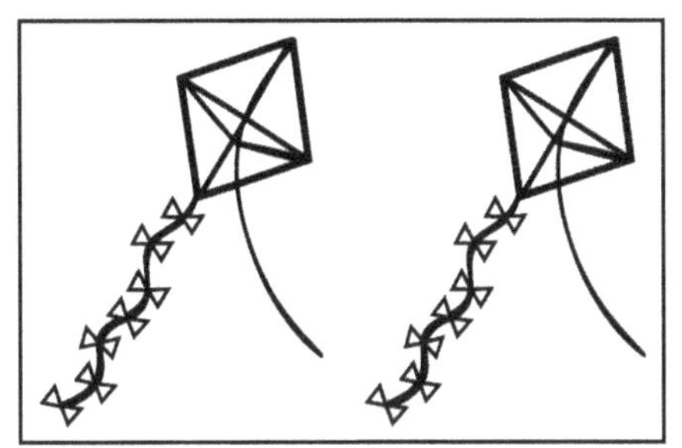

Numeral	Number Word

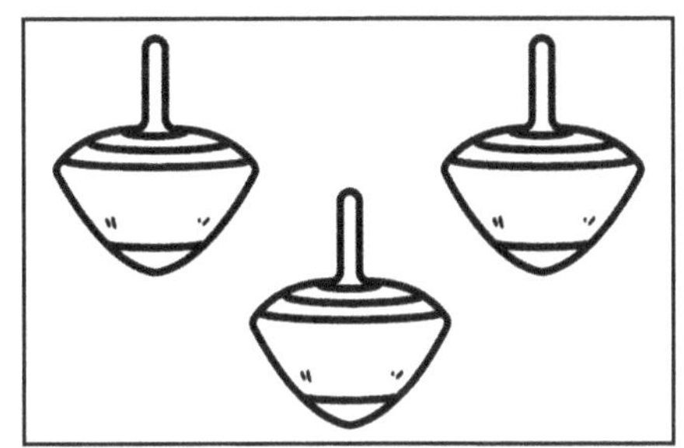

4 – four

This is the proper way to write the numeral **4**.

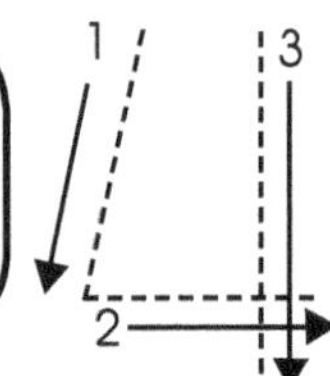

ACTIVITY 7

Practice writing the numeral **4** by tracing the broken lines. Follow the direction of the arrows.

Write more numeral **4's**. Make five sets. Leave equal spaces between the numerals.

4

Write the number word **four**. Make three sets in each row.

four

I got a/an    **today!**

(To the teacher: Encircle the hand gesture that best describes how the child worked on this activity.)

 - fairly well  - well  - very well

____

Teacher's Signature

ACTIVITY 8

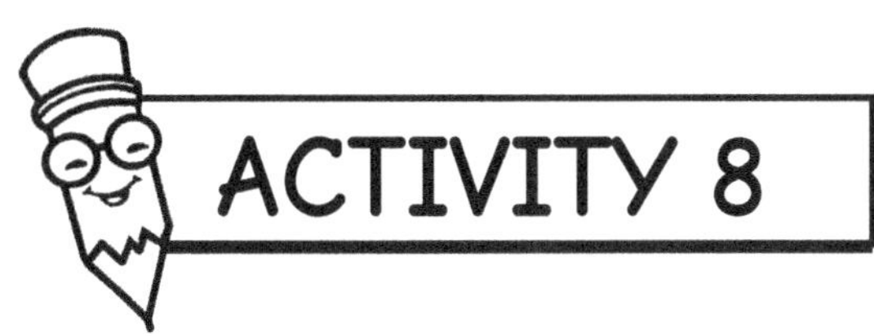

Count the objects and then write the correct numeral and number word.

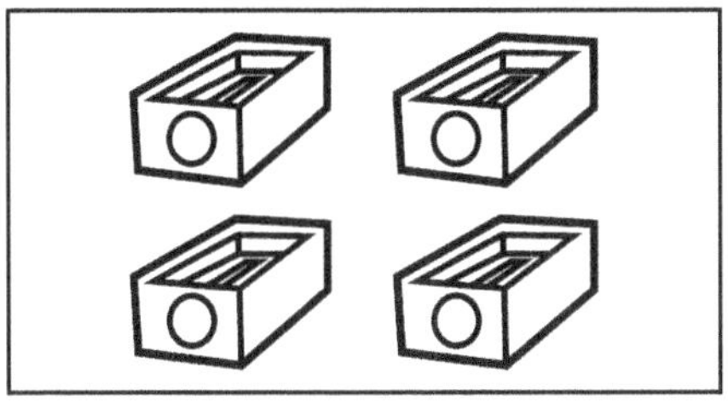

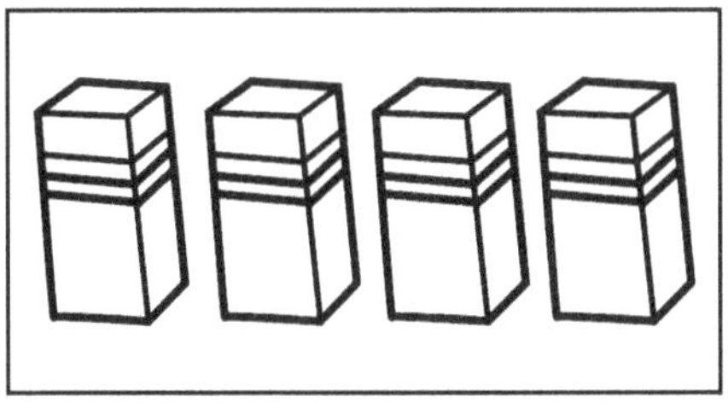

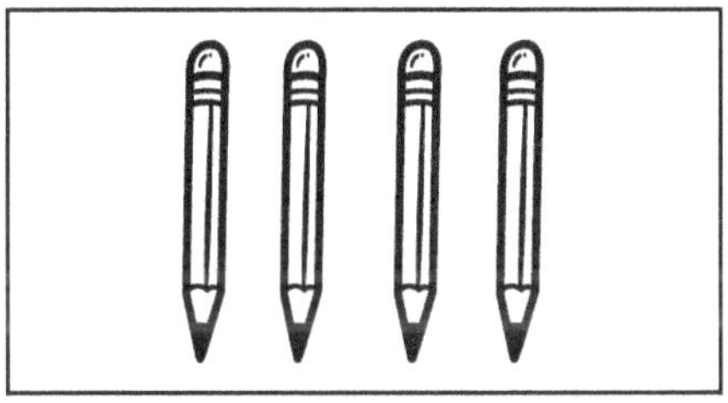

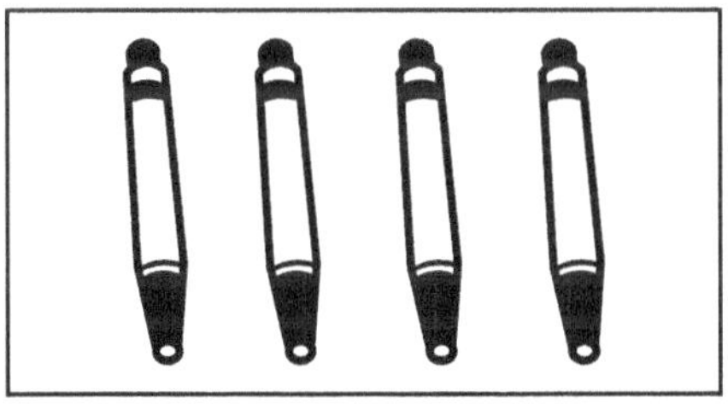

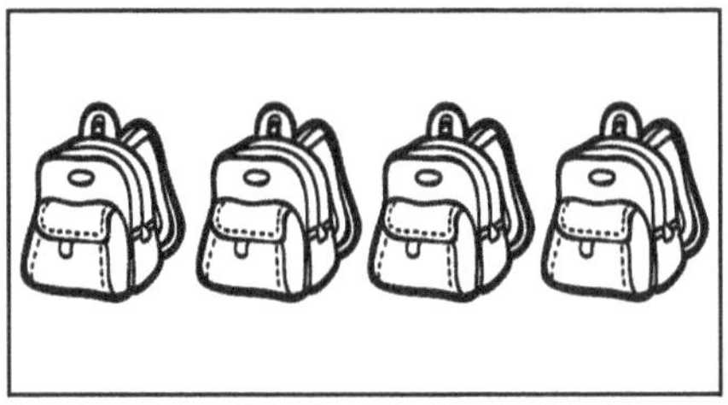

Numeral	Number Word
4	four

I got a/an 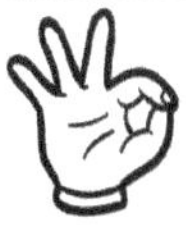 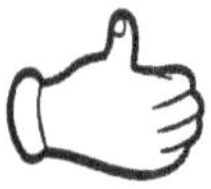 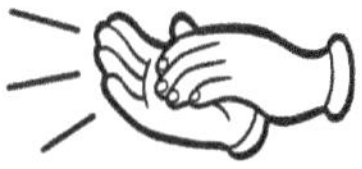 **today!**

(To the teacher: Encircle the hand gesture that best describes how the child worked on this activity.)

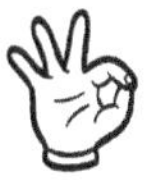 - fairly well 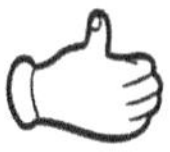 - well 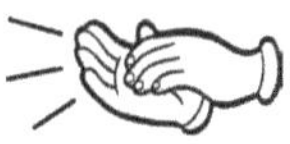 - very well

____
Teacher's Signature

5 – five

This is the proper way to write the numeral **5**.

ACTIVITY 9

Practice writing the numeral **5** by tracing the broken lines. Follow the direction of the arrows.

5 5 5 5 5

Write more numeral **5's**. Make five sets. Leave equal spaces between the numerals.

5

Write the number word **five**. Make three sets in each row.

five

I got a/an    **today!**

(To the teacher: Encircle the hand gesture that best describes how the child worked on this activity.)

 - fairly well  - well  - very well

____
Teacher's Signature

Count the objects and then write the correct numeral and number word.

	Numeral	Number Word
 (5 apples)	5	five
 (5 oranges)		
 (5 watermelons)		
 (5 strawberries)		
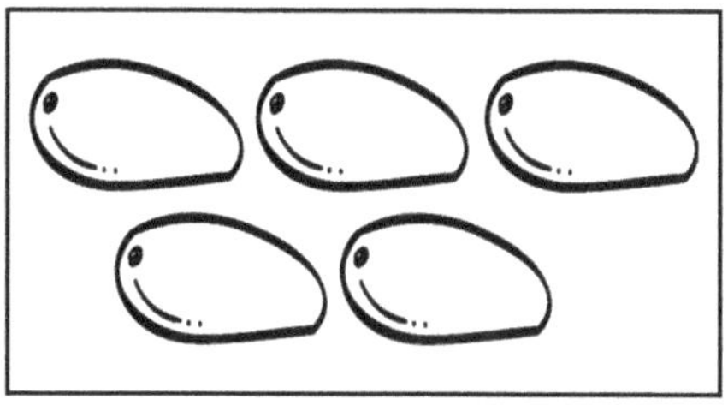 (5 mangoes)		

I got a/an (fairly well) (well) (very well) **today!**

(To the teacher: Encircle the hand gesture that best describes how the child worked on this activity.)

- fairly well  - well  - very well

Teacher's Signature

6 – six

This is the proper way to write the numeral **6**.

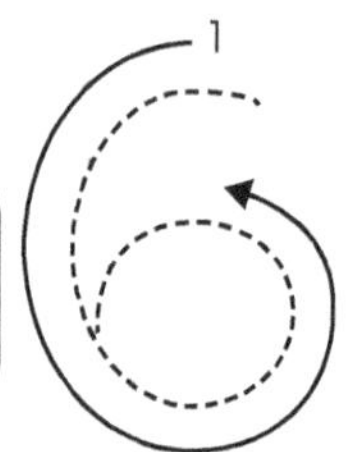

ACTIVITY 11

Practice writing the numeral **6** by tracing the broken lines. Follow the direction of the arrows.

6 6 6 6 6

Write more numeral **6's**. Make five sets. Leave equal spaces between the numerals.

6

Write the number word **six**. Make three sets in each row.

six

I got a/an    **today!**

(To the teacher: Encircle the hand gesture that best describes how the child worked on this activity.)

 - fairly well  - well  - very well

____
Teacher's Signature

ACTIVITY 12

Count the objects and then write the correct numeral and number word.

Numeral	Number Word
6	six

I got a/an ... today!

(To the teacher: Encircle the hand gesture that best describes how the child worked on this activity.)

- fairly well - well - very well

Teacher's Signature

QUIZ NO. 2 SCORE: _____

Count the objects and then write the correct numeral and number word.

Numeral	Number Word

7 – seven

This is the proper way to write the numeral **7**.

ACTIVITY 13

Practice writing the numeral **7** by tracing the broken lines. Follow the direction of the arrows.

7 7 7 7 7

Write more numeral **7's**. Make five sets. Leave equal spaces between the numerals.

7

Write the number word **seven**. Make three sets in each row.

seven

I got a/an [fairly well] [well] [very well] **today!**

(To the teacher: Encircle the hand gesture that best describes how the child worked on this activity.)

- fairly well - well - very well

____
Teacher's Signature

ACTIVITY 14

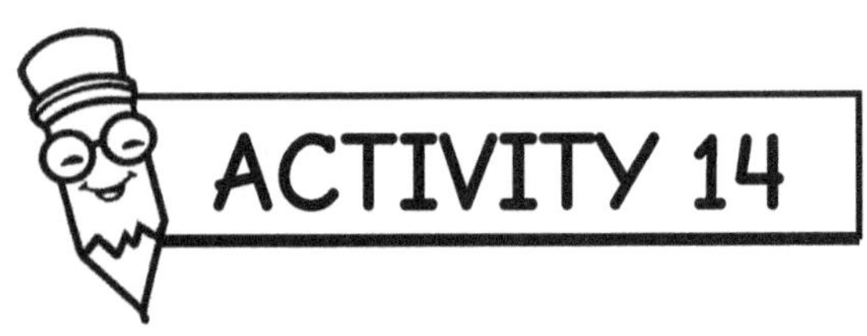

Count the objects and then write the correct numeral and number word.

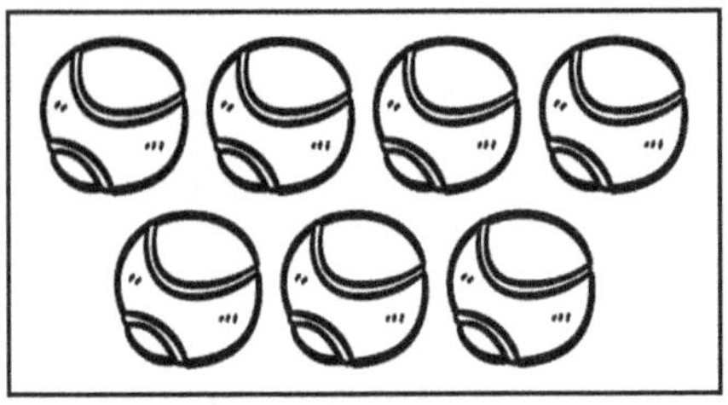

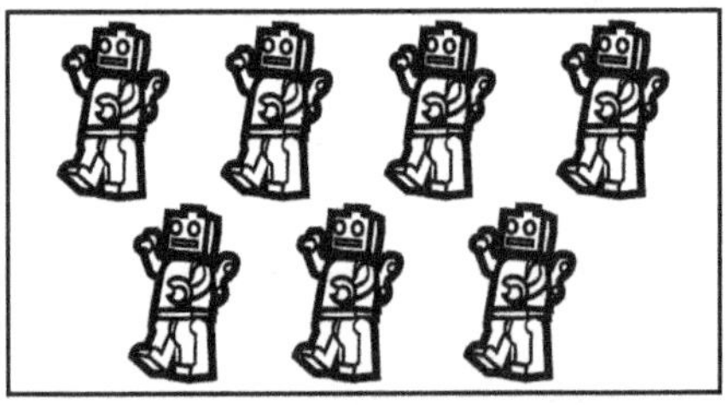

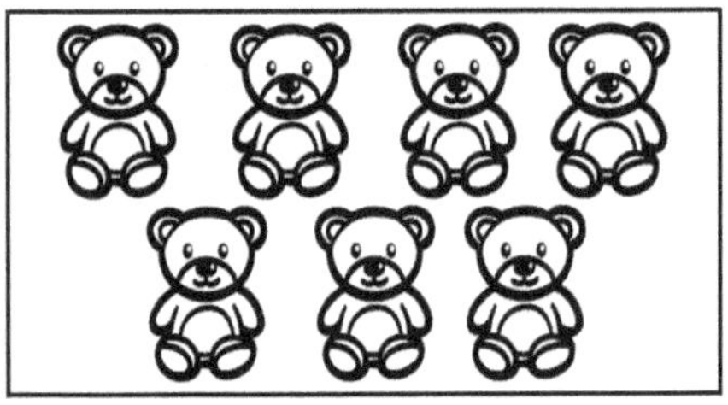

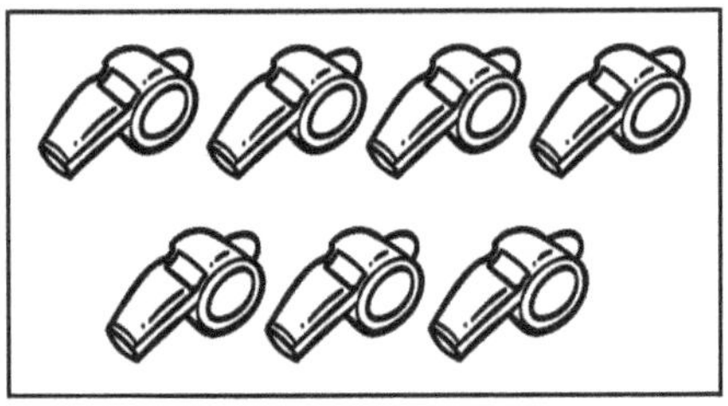

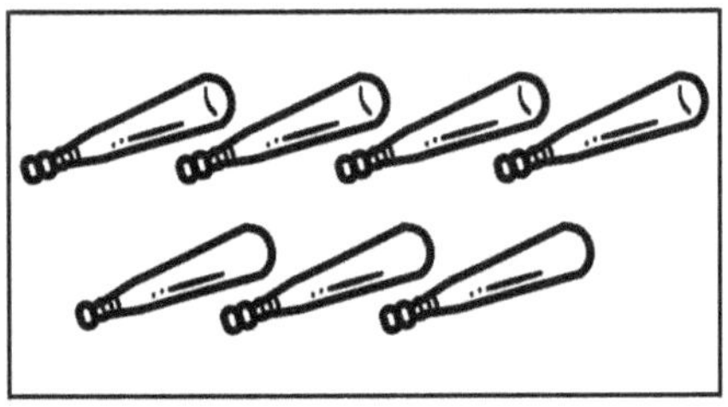

Numeral	Number Word
7	seven

I got a/an 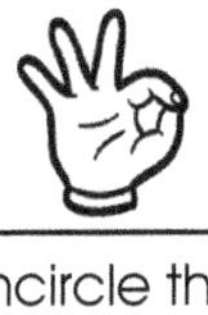 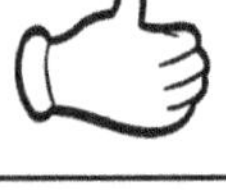 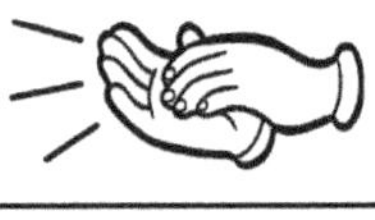 **today!**

(To the teacher: Encircle the hand gesture that best describes how the child worked on this activity.)

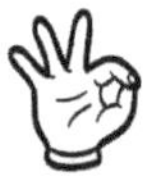 - fairly well 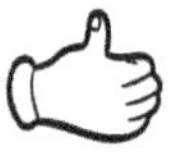 - well 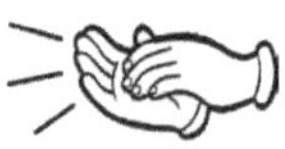 - very well

____

Teacher's Signature

8 – eight

This is the proper way to write the numeral **8**.

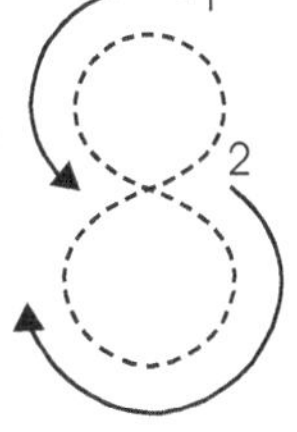

ACTIVITY 15

Practice writing the numeral **8** by tracing the broken lines. Follow the direction of the arrows.

Write more numeral **8's**. Make five sets. Leave equal spaces between the numerals.

8

Write the number word **eight**. Make three sets in each row.

eight

I got a/an **today!**

(To the teacher: Encircle the hand gesture that best describes how the child worked on this activity.)

- fairly well - well - very well

Teacher's Signature

ACTIVITY 16

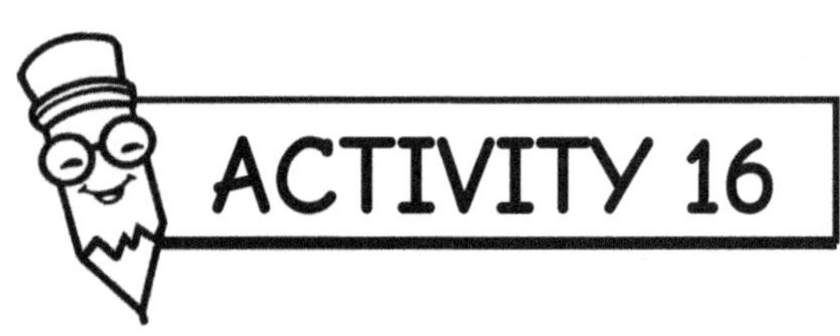

Count the objects and then write the correct numeral and number word.

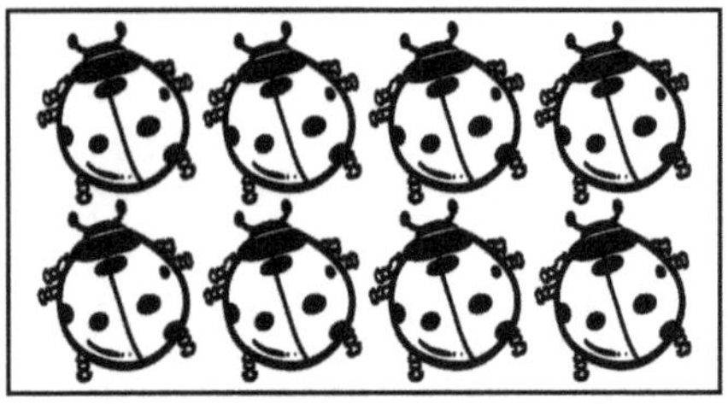

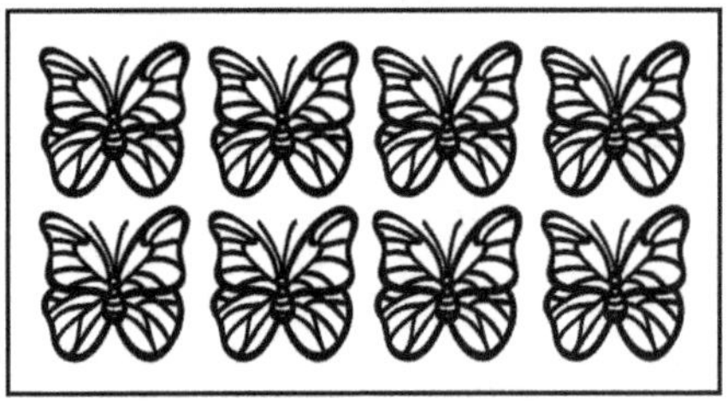

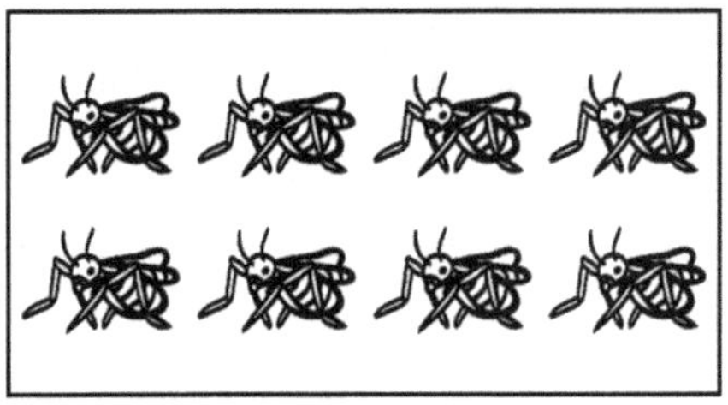

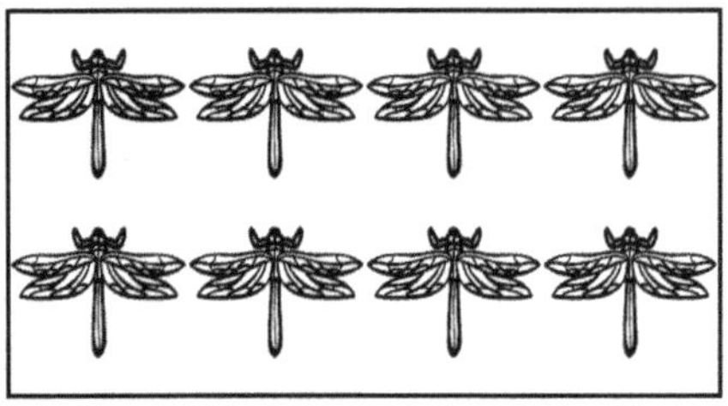

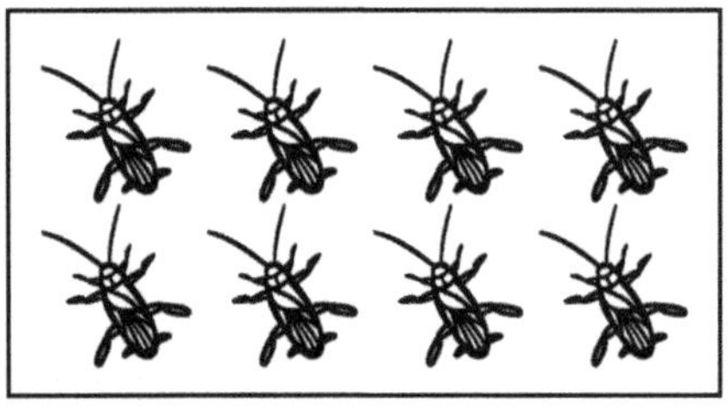

Numeral	Number Word
8	eight

I got a/an 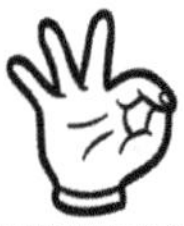 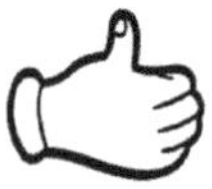 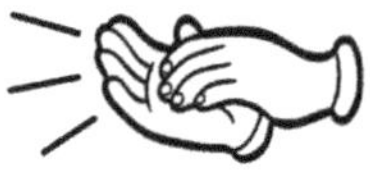 **today!**

(To the teacher: Encircle the hand gesture that best describes how the child worked on this activity.)

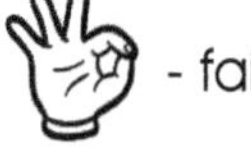

 - fairly well - well - very well

____

Teacher's Signature

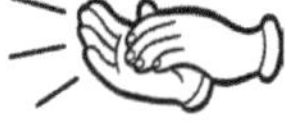

9 – nine

This is the proper way to write the numeral **9**.

ACTIVITY 17

Practice writing the numeral **9** by tracing the broken lines. Follow the direction of the arrows.

Write more numeral **9's**. Make five sets. Leave equal spaces between the numerals.

9

Write the number word **nine**. Make three sets in each row.

nine

I got a/an    **today!**

(To the teacher: Encircle the hand gesture that best describes how the child worked on this activity.)

 - fairly well  - well  - very well

____
Teacher's Signature

ACTIVITY 18

Count the objects and then write the correct numeral and number word.

Numeral	Number Word
 9	nine

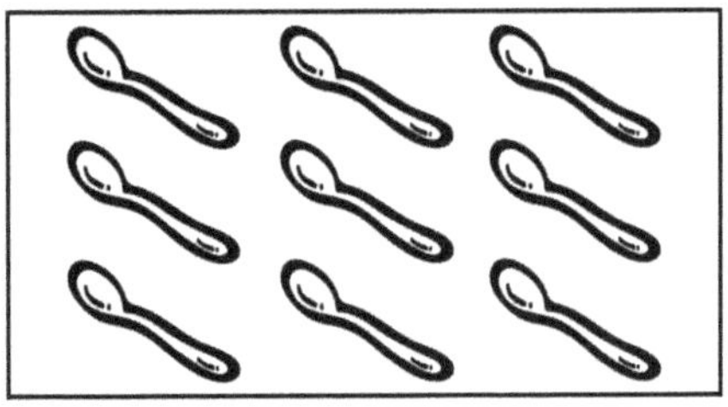

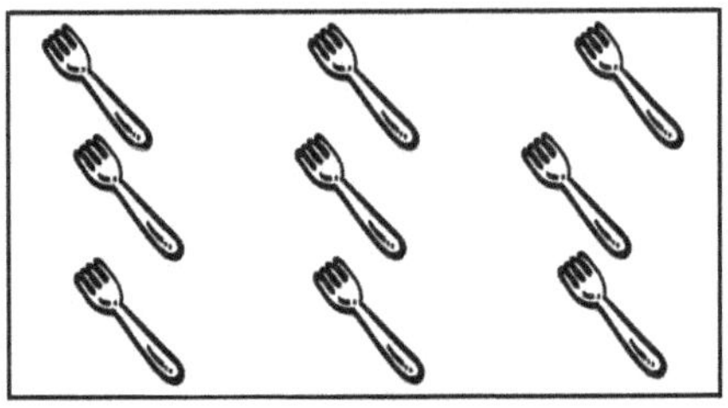

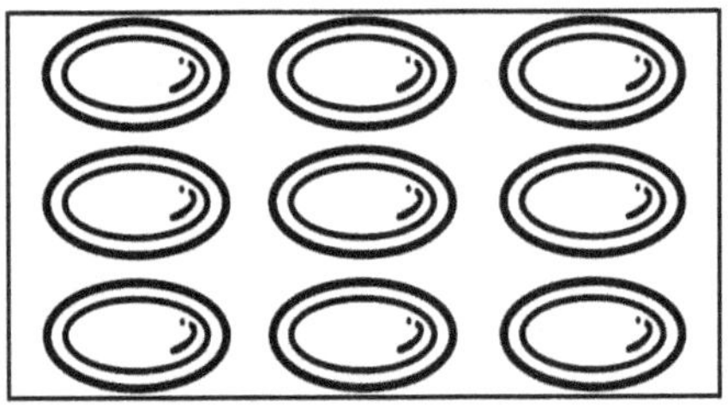

I got a/an today!

(To the teacher: Encircle the hand gesture that best describes how the child worked on this activity.)

 - fairly well  - well  - very well

Teacher's Signature

10 – ten

This is the proper way to write the numeral **10**.

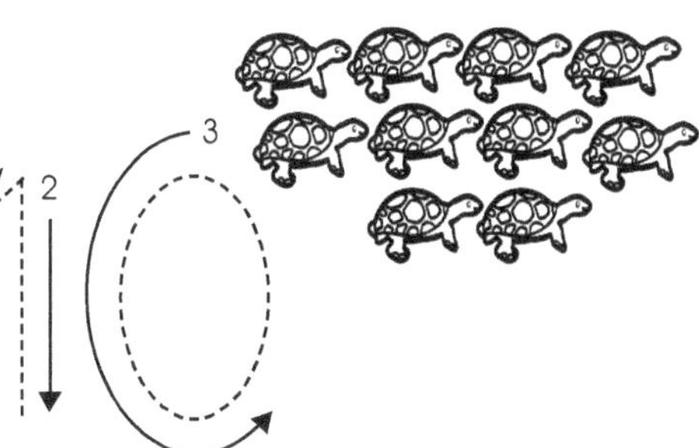

ACTIVITY 19

Practice writing the numeral **10** by tracing the broken lines. Follow the direction of the arrows.

10 10 10 10

Write more numeral **10's.** Make five sets. Leave equal spaces between the numerals.

10

Write the number word **ten**. Make three sets in each row.

ten

I got a/an    **today!**

(To the teacher: Encircle the hand gesture that best describes how the child worked on this activity.)

 - fairly well  - well  - very well

Teacher's Signature

ACTIVITY 20

Count the objects and then write the correct numeral and number word.

Numeral	Number Word
10	ten

I got a/an [hand gestures] **today!**

(To the teacher: Encircle the hand gesture that best describes how the child worked on this activity.)

 - fairly well  - well  - very well

____

Teacher's Signature

QUIZ NO. 3 SCORE: ______

Write the numeral and number word for each set of objects.

Numeral	Number Word

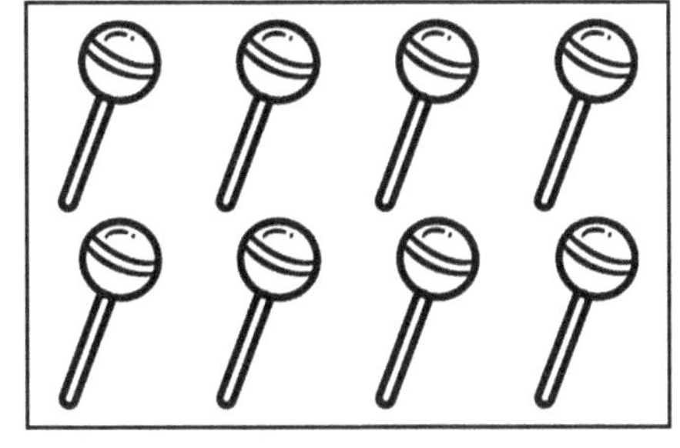

Numeral	Number Word

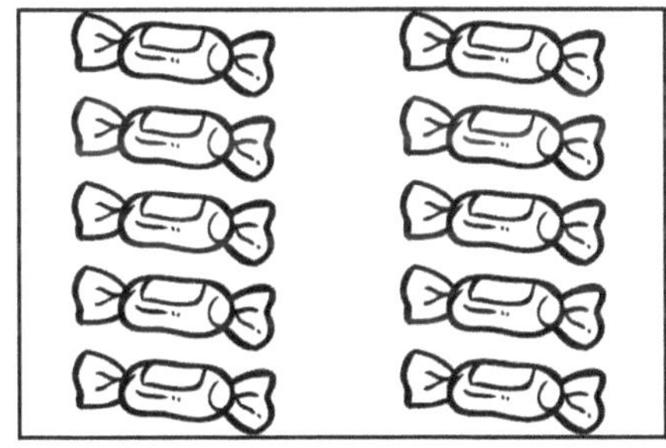

Numeral	Number Word

Numeral	Number Word

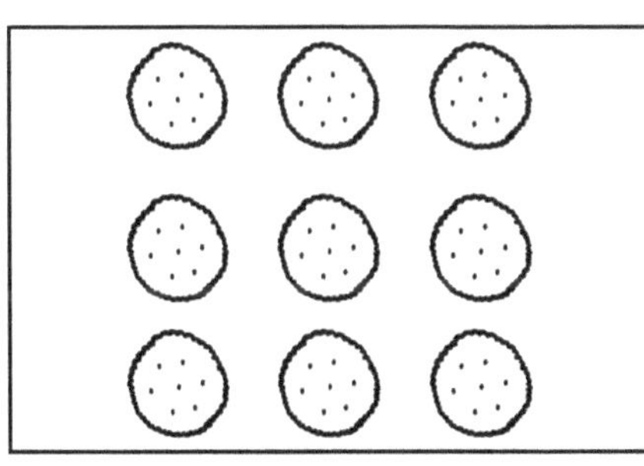

Numeral	Number Word

Write the numerals 1 to 100 on the lines, with ten numerals in each row. Follow the proper strokes in writing numerals, leaving equal spaces in between.

I got a/an today!

(To the teacher: Encircle the hand gesture that best describes how the child worked on this activity.)

- fairly well - well - very well

Teacher's Signature

LESSON 2

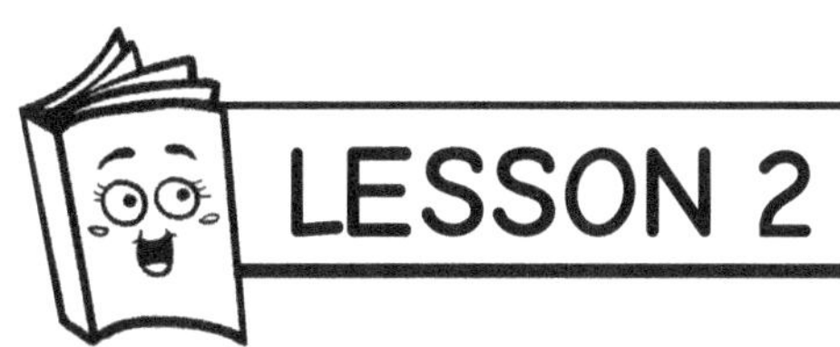

COPYING NAMES AND WORDS
Animals

ACTIVITY 22

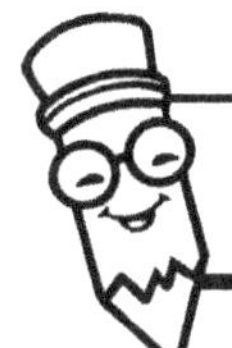

Copy the names of animals.

antelope

beaver

chicken

dolphin

eagle

flamingo

giraffe

horse

iguana

jaguar

koala

lobster

mole

newt

otter

parrot

quetzal

raccoon

stingray

toad

umbrellabird

vulture

walrus

xylophage

yak

zebra

(To the teacher: Encircle the hand gesture that best describes how the child worked on this activity.)

 - fairly well  - well  - very well

____

Teacher's Signature

LESSON 3 COLORS

ACTIVITY 23

Copy the names of colors on the lines twice. Leave equal spaces between words.

red

yellow

blue

orange

green

violet

brown

black

white

pink

indigo

I got a/an    **today!**

(To the teacher: Encircle the hand gesture that best describes how the child worked on this activity.)

- fairly well  - well  - very well

Teacher's Signature

FAMILY MEMBERS

Copy the name of each family member beside the correct picture.

father

mother

brother

sister

baby

grandfather

grandmother

aunt

uncle

cousins

I got a/an    today!

(To the teacher: Encircle the hand gesture that best describes how the child worked on this activity.)

- fairly well  - well  - very well

Teacher's Signature

DAYS OF THE WEEK

Copy the names of the days of the week on the lines.

Sunday

Monday

Tuesday

Wednesday

Thursday

Friday

Saturday

I got a/an **today!**

(To the teacher: Encircle the hand gesture that best describes how the child worked on this activity.)

 - fairly well  - well  - very well

____

Teacher's Signature

MONTHS OF THE YEAR

Copy the names of the months of the year on the lines.

January

February

March

April

May

June

July

August

September

October

November

December

I got a/an    today!

(To the teacher: Encircle the hand gesture that best describes how the child worked on this activity.)

- fairly well  - well  - very well

____
Teacher's Signature

LESSON 7 ACTION WORDS

ACTIVITY 27

Copy each action word before the correct picture.

laugh

write

mix

walk

cry

touch

think

swim

quiver

celebrate

I got a/an today!

(To the teacher: Encircle the hand gesture that best describes how the child worked on this activity.)

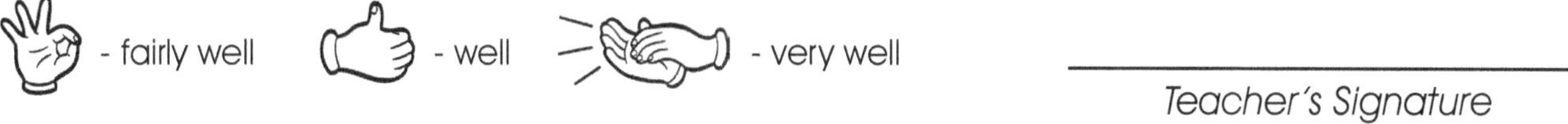

Teacher's Signature

LESSON 8 DESCRIBING WORDS

ACTIVITY 28

Copy each describing word beside the correct picture.

bright

crowded

wrong

heavy

wealthy

excited

skinny

dirty

dark

thick

clean

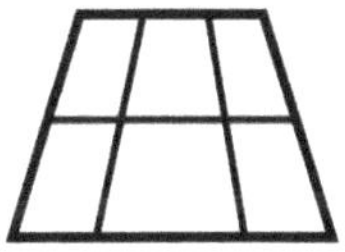

rough

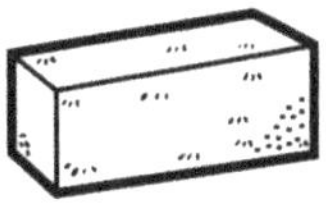

I got a/an    **today!**

(To the teacher: Encircle the hand gesture that best describes how the child worked on this activity.)

- fairly well  - well  - very well

Teacher's Signature

PROGRESS CHART
SECOND QUARTER

NAME: ______________________ LEVEL: ____________

Activity	What I Got			Quiz	No. of Items	My Score
	(fairly well)	(well)	(very well)			
1				1	5	
2				2	5	
3				3	5	
4						
5						
6						
7						
8						
9						
10						
11						
12						
13						
14						
15						
16						
17						
18						
19						
20						
21						
22						
23						
24						
25						
26						
27						
28						
TOTAL				TOTAL	15	

______________________ ______________________

Parent's/Guardian's Signature Teacher's Signature

Legend: fairly well well very well

THIRD QUARTER

Teacher's Objectives and Student Evaluation

Lesson	*At the end of the activities, the child should be able to:*			
1	1. copy names of things used and seen at home on lined paper			
	2. write words legibly			
2	3. copy names of the different rooms in the house on lined paper			
3	4. copy names of things used and seen in school on lined paper			
4	5. copy the names of the different places in school on lined paper			
5	6. copy names of our school helpers			
	7. master the spelling of the names of our school helpers			
6	8. copy the names of the different places in the community on lined paper			
	9. be familiarized with the places in the community			
7	10. copy the names of our community helpers on lined paper			
	11. master the spelling of the names of our community helpers			
8	12. copy names of places on lined paper, leaving enough space between words			
	13. write words with uppercase and lowercase letters legibly			
9	14. copy names of people on lined paper, leaving enough space in between			
10	15. copy phrases on lined paper, leaving enough space between words			
11	16. copy different titles on lined paper, observing enough spacing between words			
	17. write words with uppercase and lowercase letters legibly			
12	18. copy sentences on lined paper, putting emphasis on proper spacing between words			
13	19. copy paragraphs on lined paper, emphasizing on proper spacing between words and sentences			
14	20. copy a sample homework on lined paper similar to a writing notebook			
	21. copy homeworks and lectures on a writing notebook			
	22. write legibly			

Legend:  fairly well  well  very well

LESSON 1

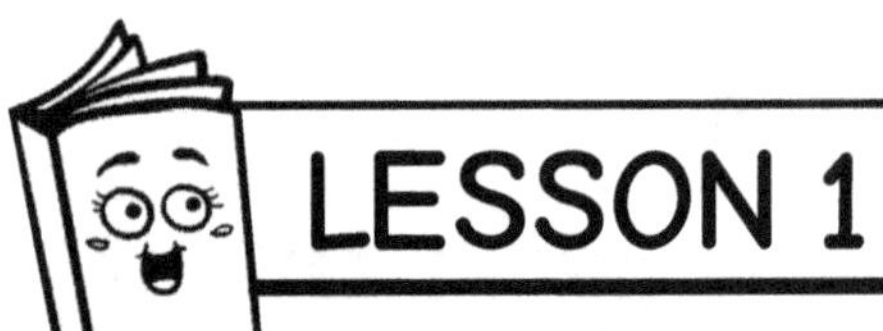

COPYING OTHER NAMES AND WORDS

ACTIVITY 1

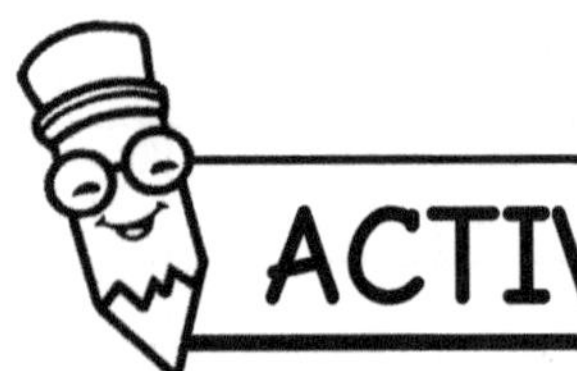

Things Used and Seen at Home

Copy the names of things we use at home on the lines below each picture.

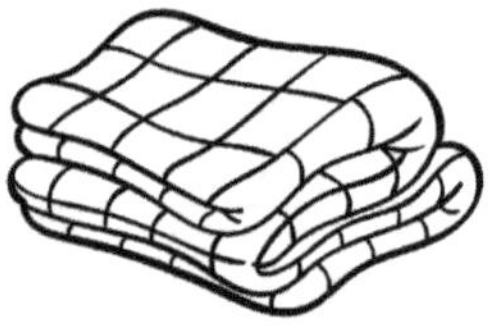

blanket

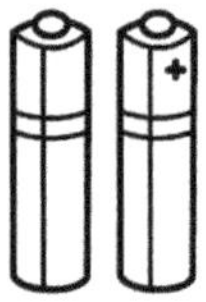

battery

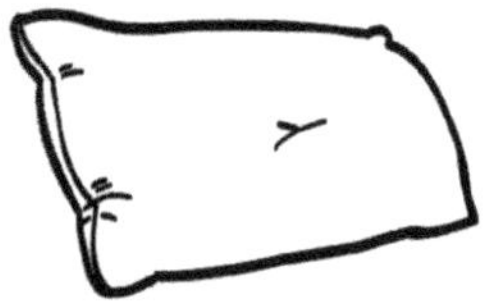

pillow

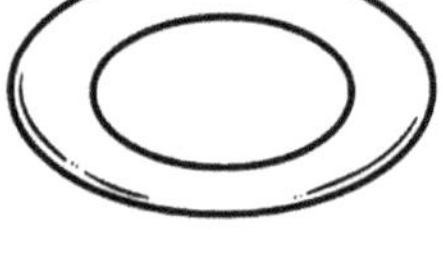

plate

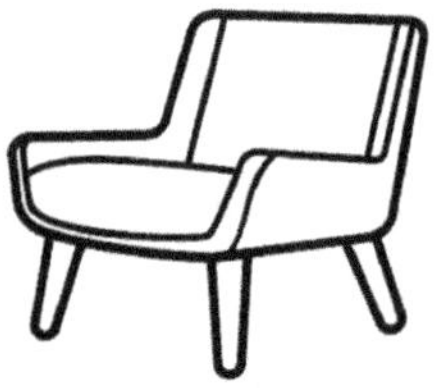

chair

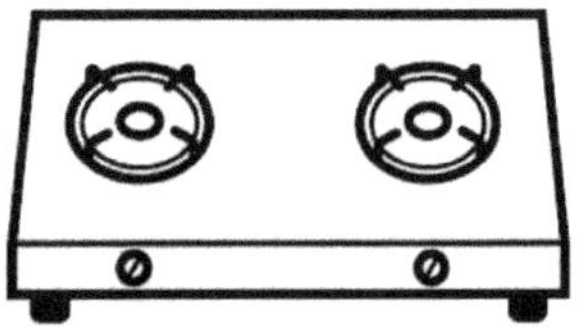

stove

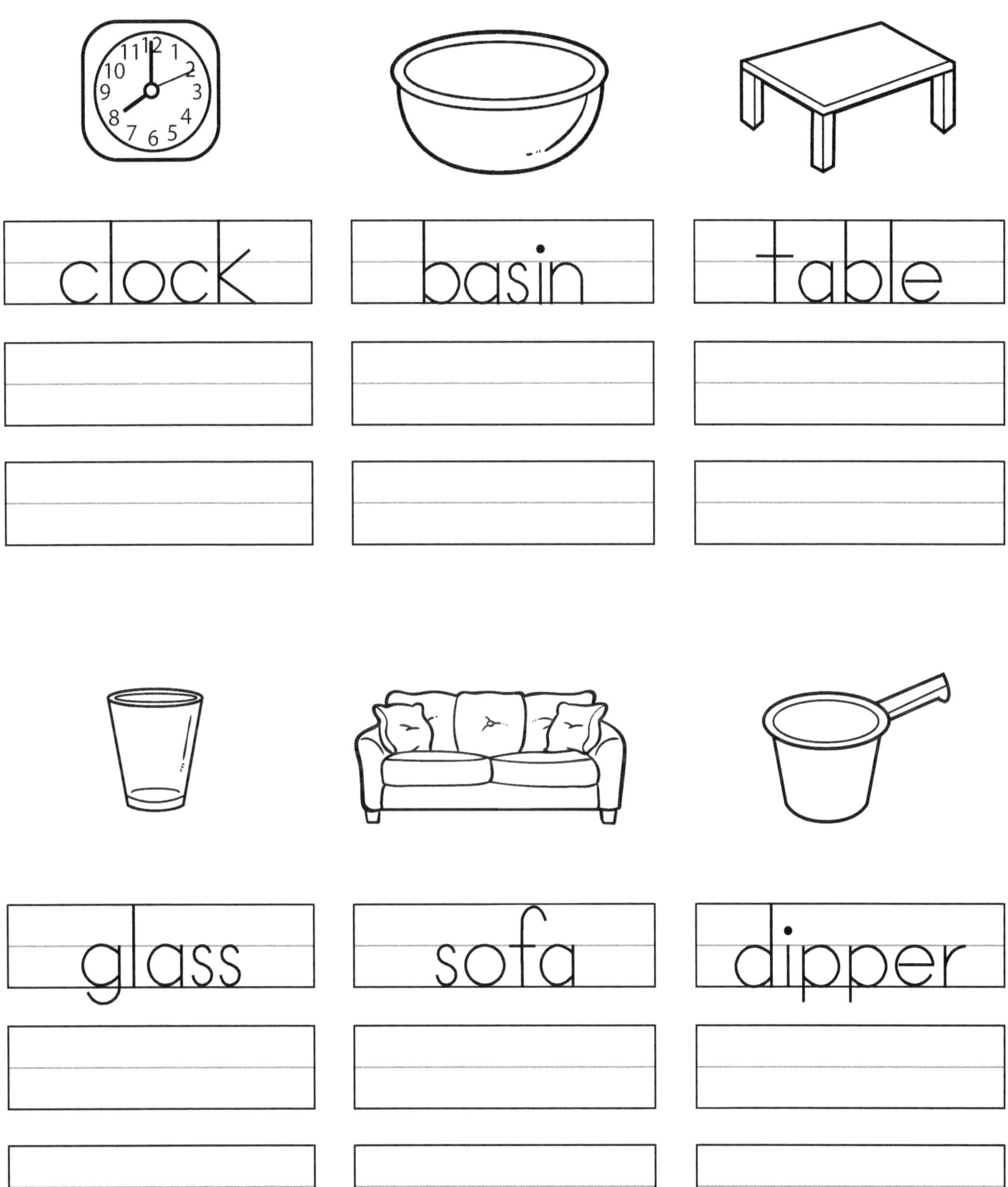

clock
basin
table
glass
sofa
dipper

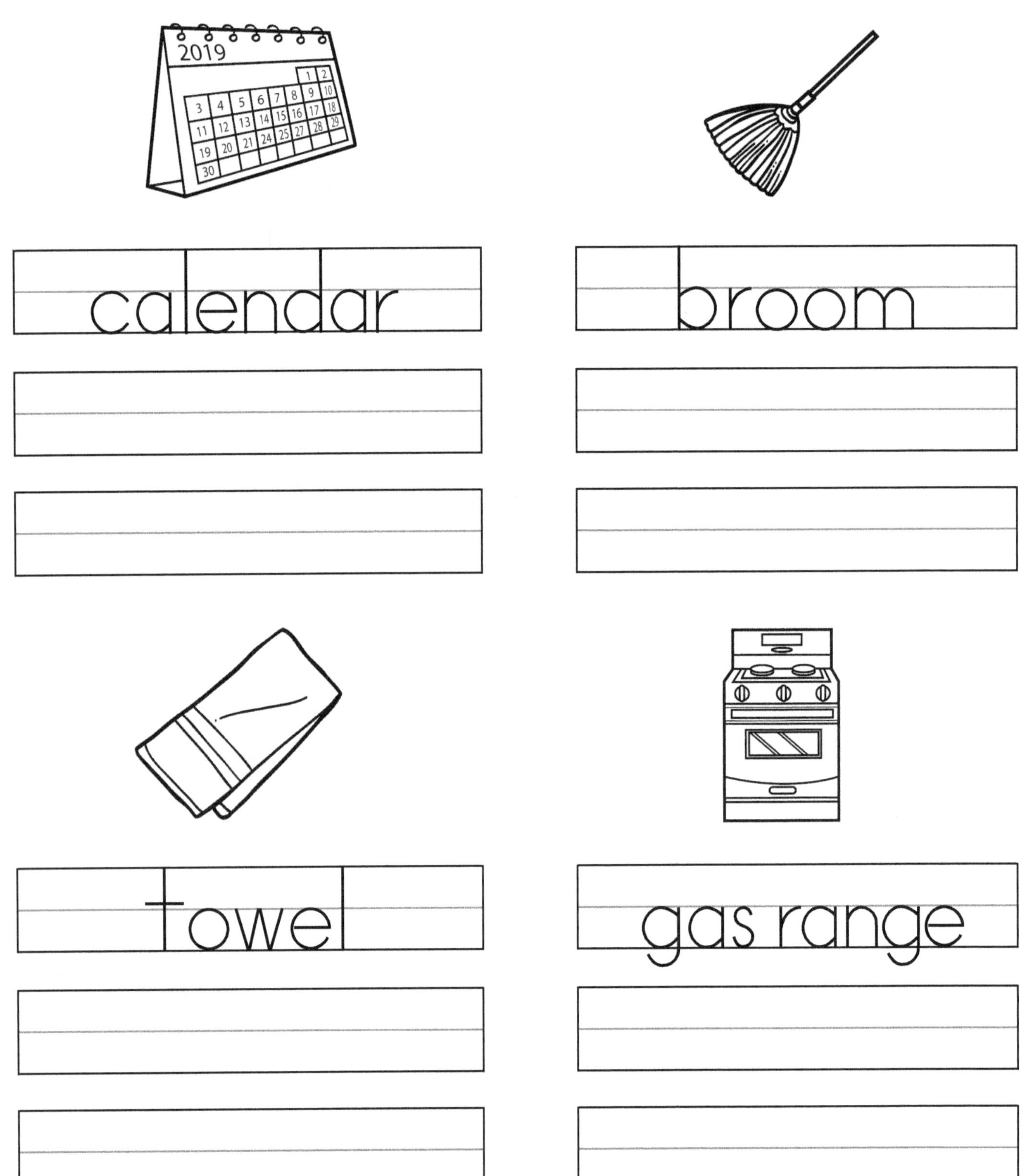
calendar
broom
towel
gas range

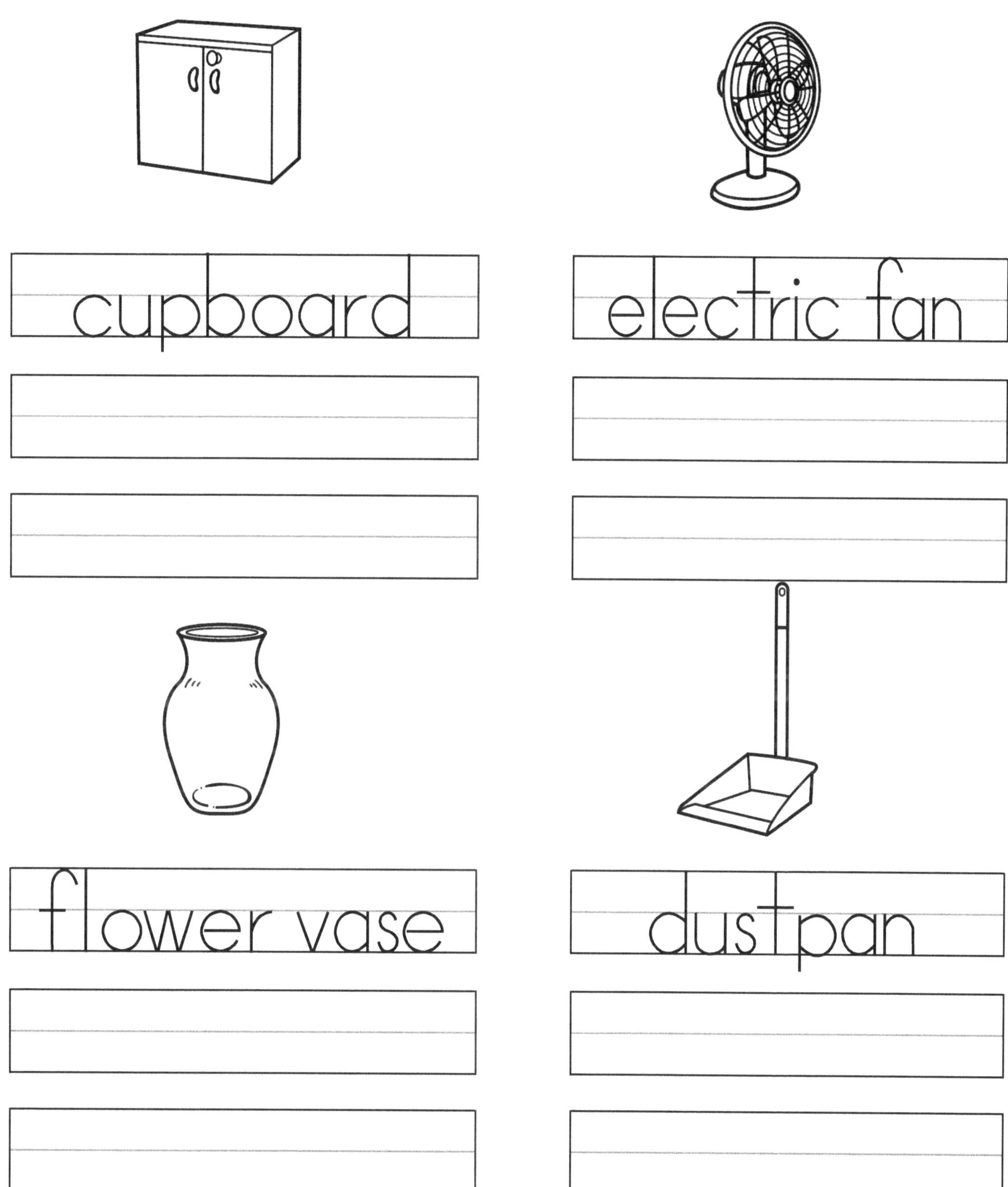

cupboard

electric fan

flower vase

dustpan

trash can

hanger

refrigerator

pitcher

I got a/an    today!

(To the teacher: Encircle the hand gesture that best describes how the child worked on this activity.)

 - fairly well  - well  - very well

Teacher's Signature

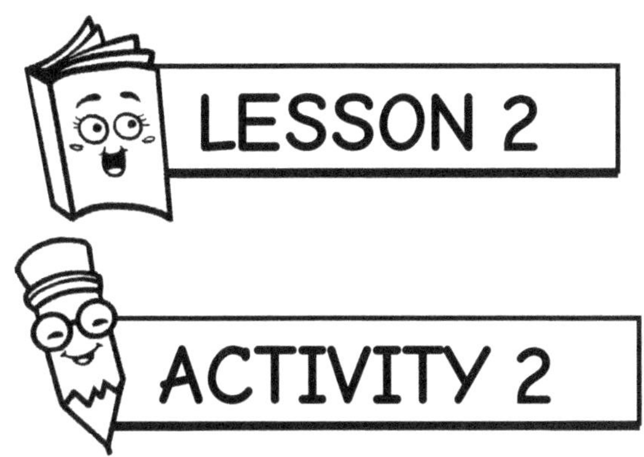

ROOMS AND SPACES IN THE HOUSE

Copy the names of the different rooms in the house on the lines below each picture.

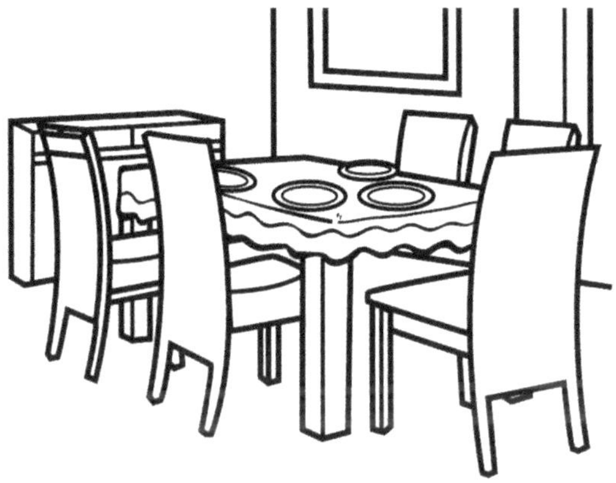

dining room

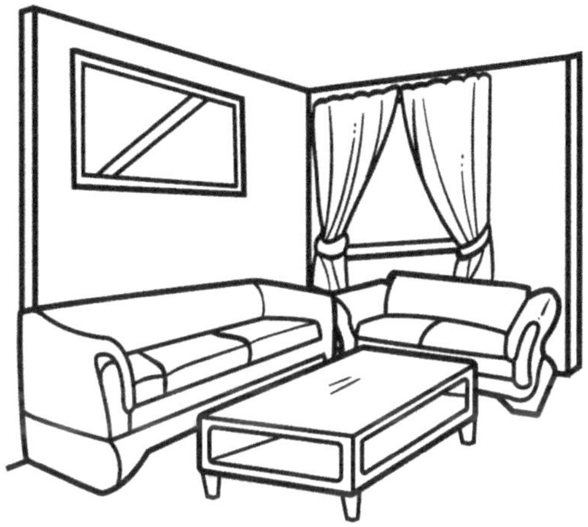

living room

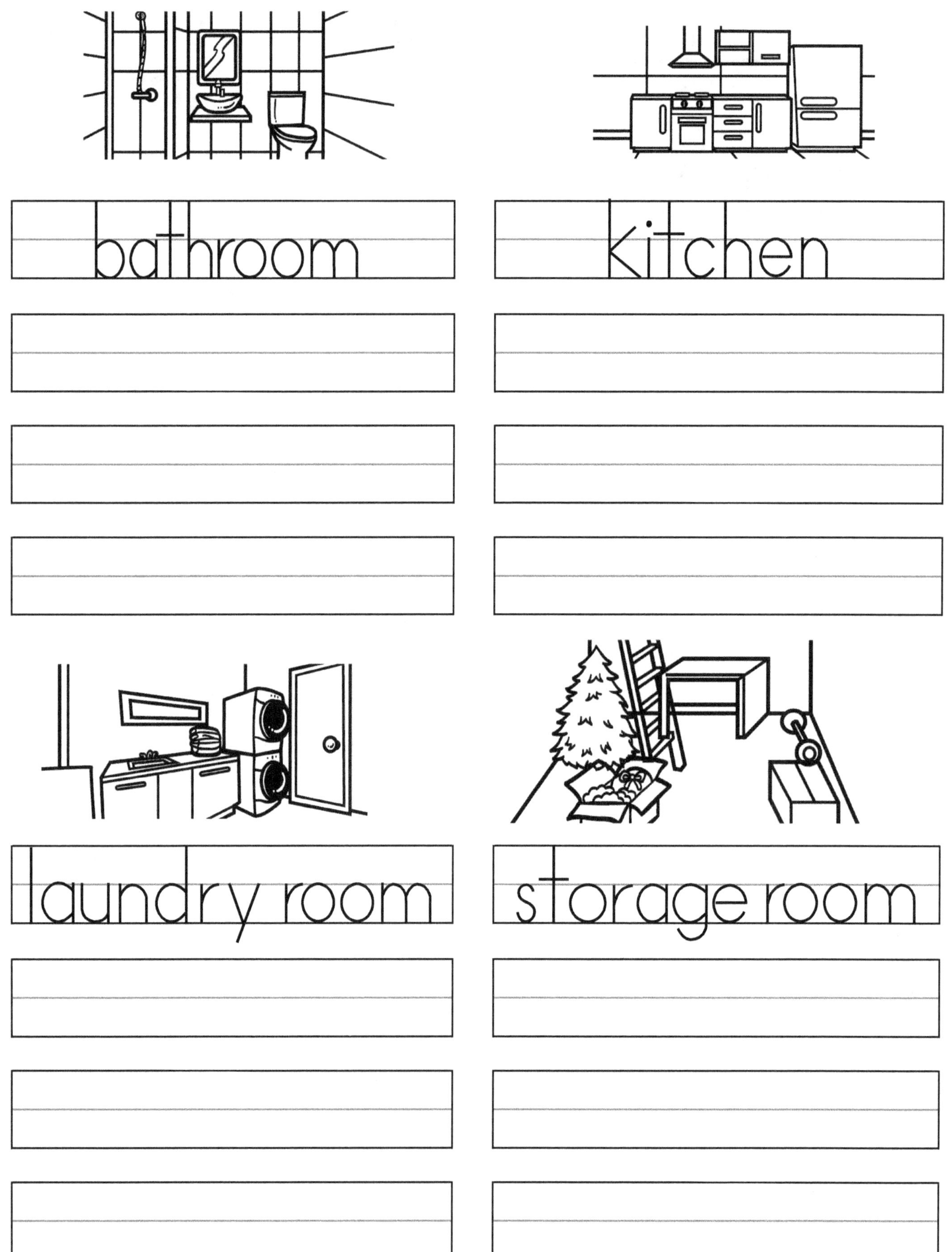
bathroom
kitchen
laundry room
storage room

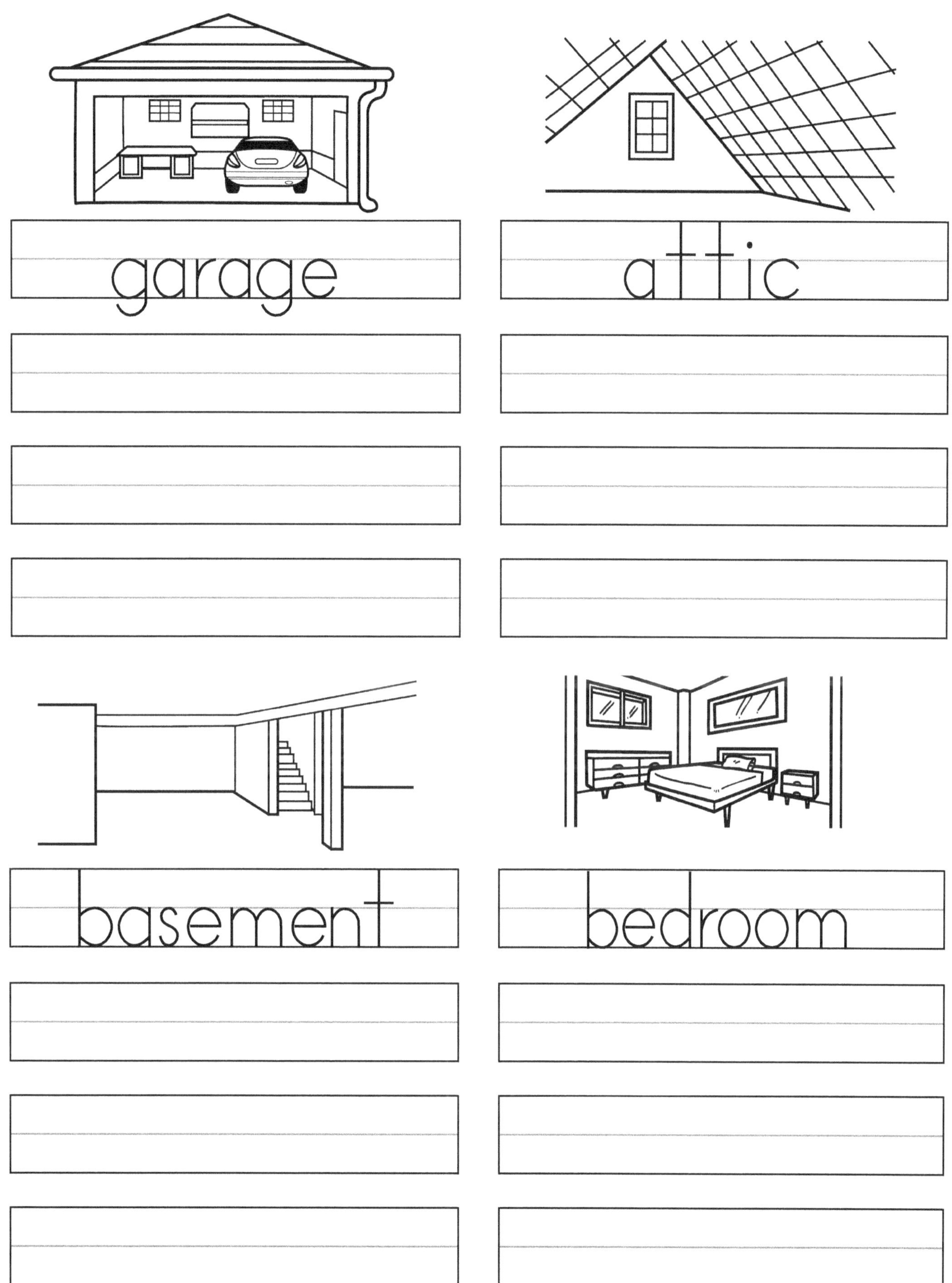
garage
attic
basement
bedroom

study room

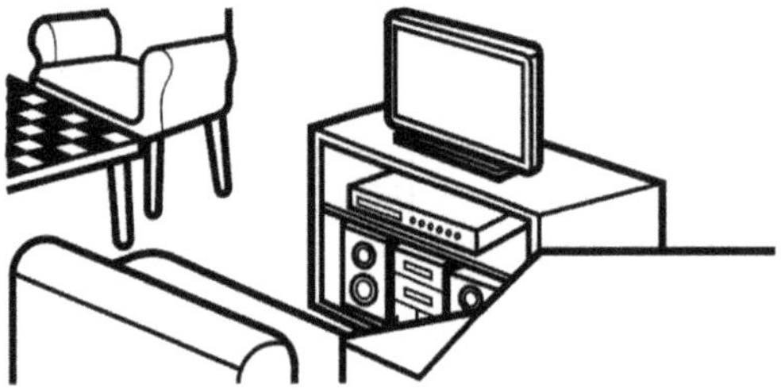

recreation room

I got a/an  today!

(To the teacher: Encircle the hand gesture that best describes how the child worked on this activity.)

 - fairly well  - well  - very well

Teacher's Signature

LESSON 3 THINGS USED AND SEEN IN SCHOOL

ACTIVITY 3

Copy the names of things used and seen in school on the lines below each picture.

marker

eraser

pencil

ballpen

ruler

scissors

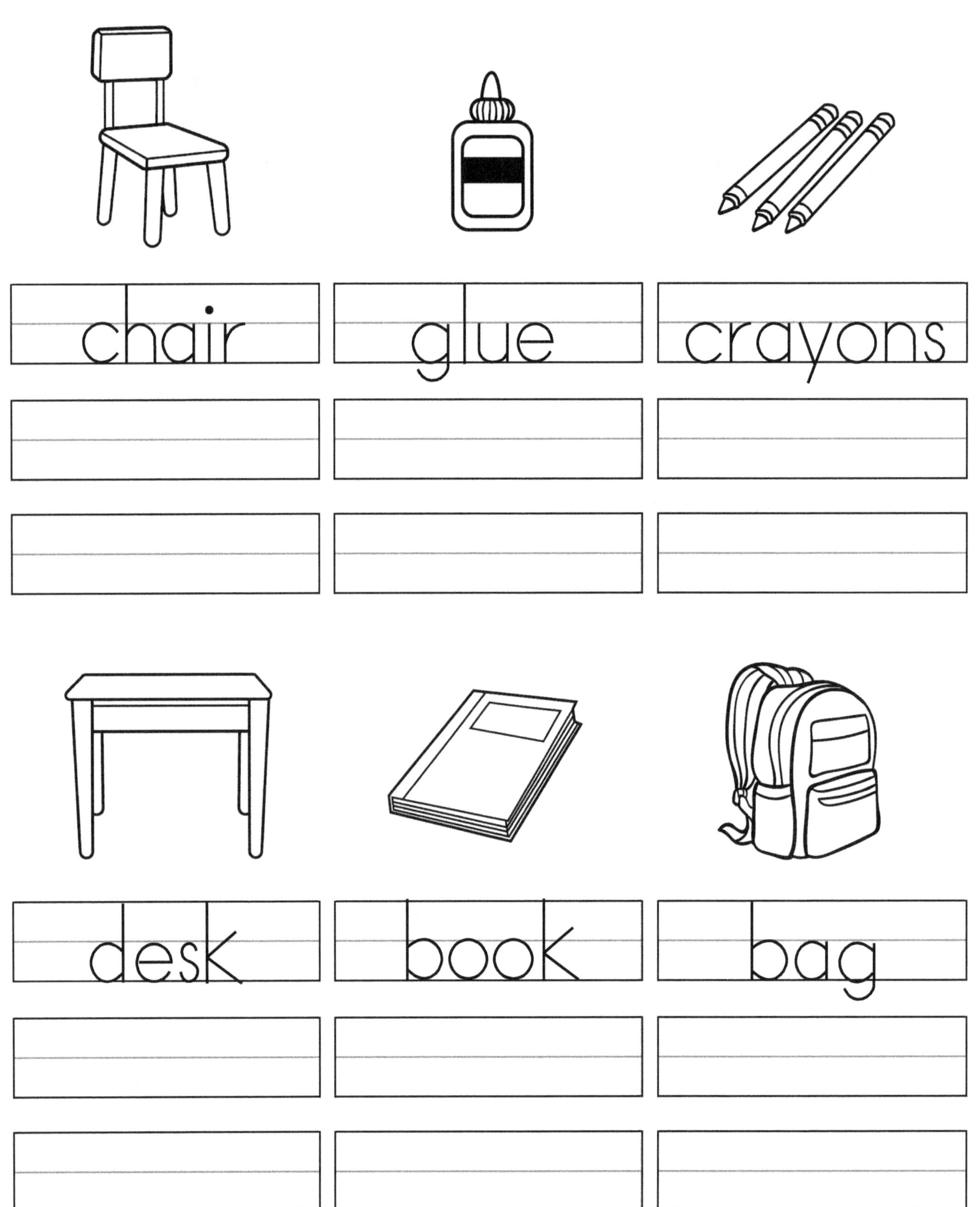
chair
glue
crayons
desk
book
bag

COLORED PENCILS
white board
colored pencils
lunch box
paper clip

(To the teacher: Encircle the hand gesture that best describes how the child worked on this activity.)

- fairly well - well - very well

Teacher's Signature

PLACES IN SCHOOL

Copy the names of the places in school below each picture.

library

office

classroom

playground

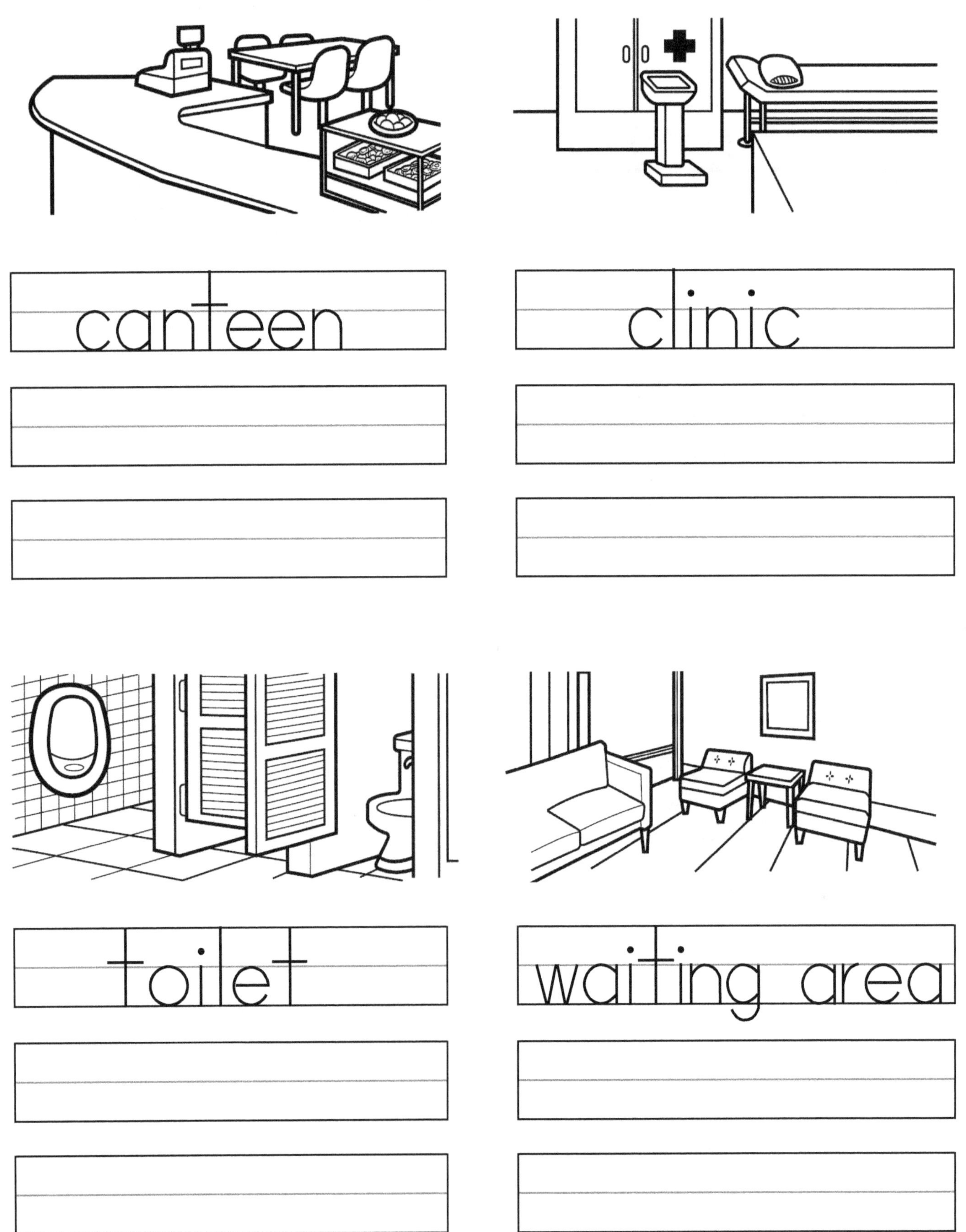
canteen
clinic
toilet
waiting area

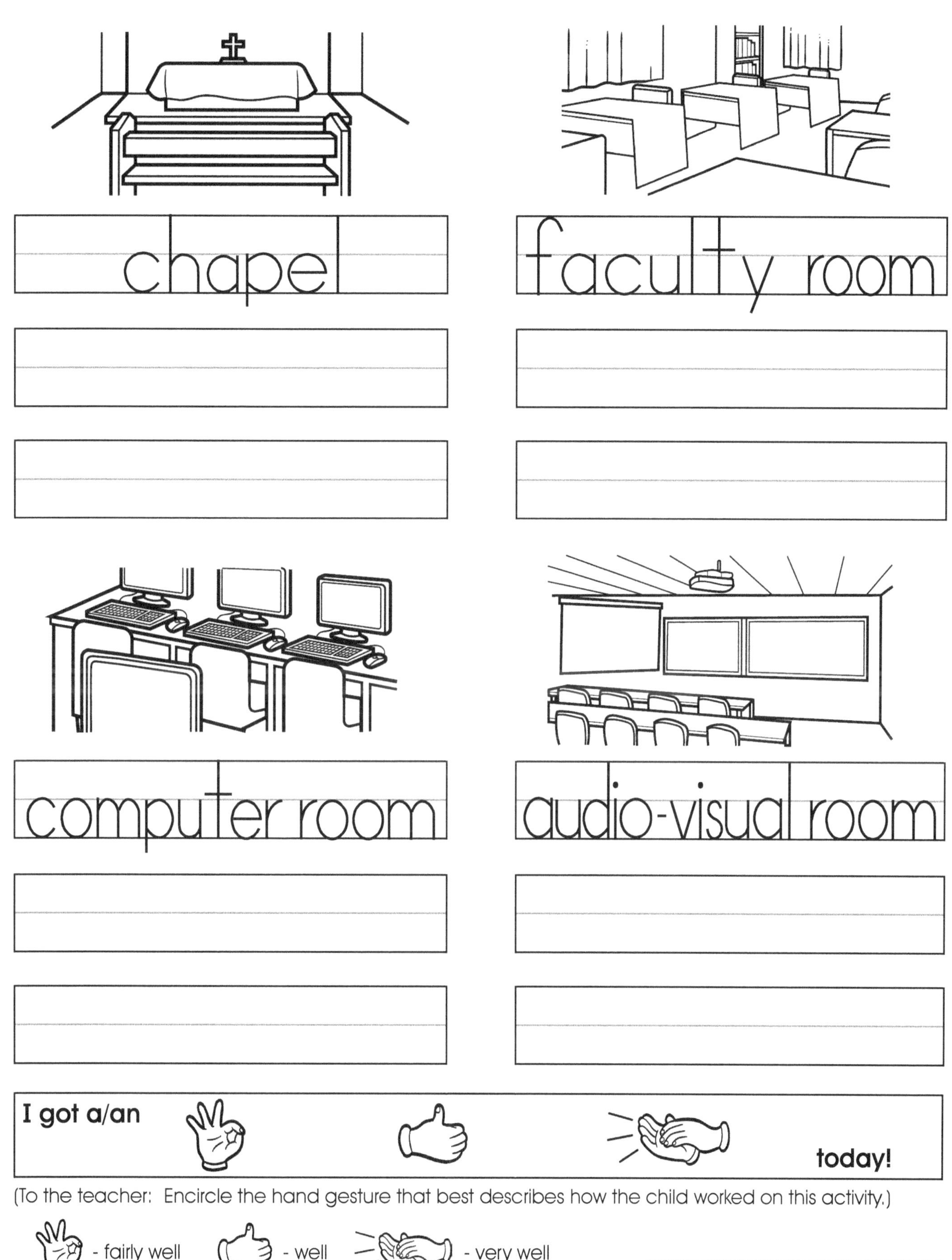

(To the teacher: Encircle the hand gesture that best describes how the child worked on this activity.)

- fairly well - well - very well

Teacher's Signature

LESSON 5 SCHOOL HELPERS

ACTIVITY 5

Copy the names of our school helpers on the lines below each picture.

teacher

principal

registrar

librarian

security guard

janitor

nurse

food server

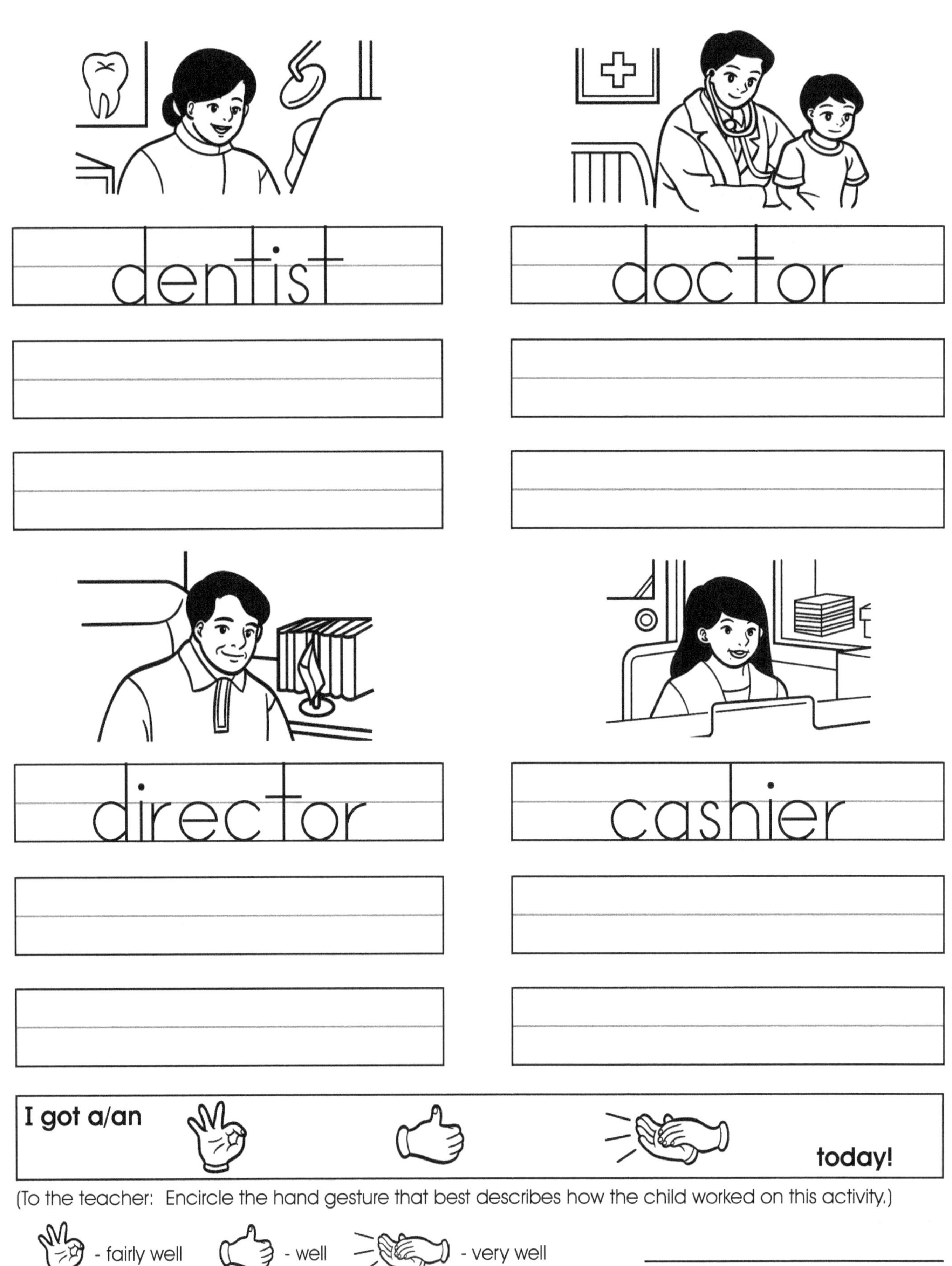

(To the teacher: Encircle the hand gesture that best describes how the child worked on this activity.)

- fairly well - well - very well

Teacher's Signature

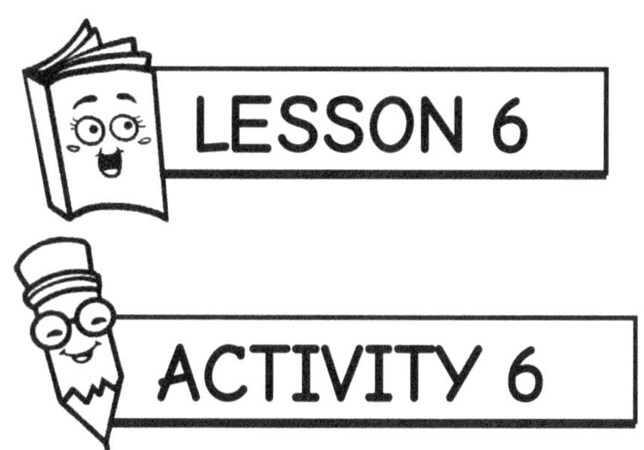

PLACES IN THE COMMUNITY

Copy the names of places in the community on the lines below each picture.

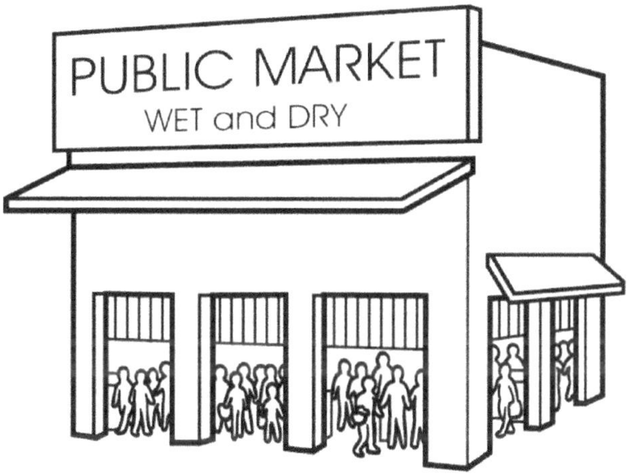

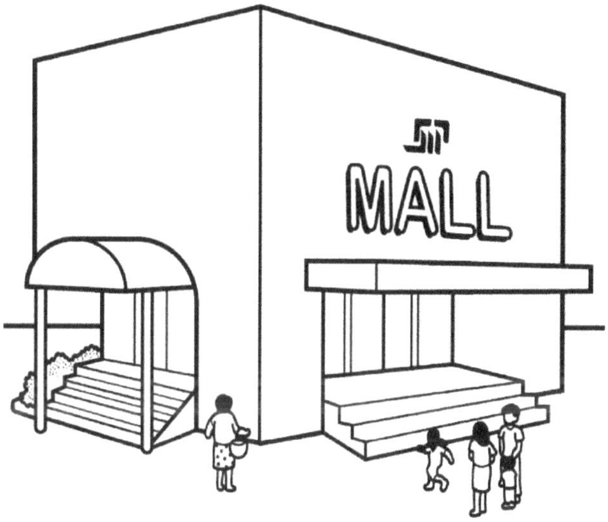

market	mall

BABIANO
LEARNING SCHOOL
HOSPITAL
school
hospital
HDJ DRUGSTORE
PARK
drugstore
park

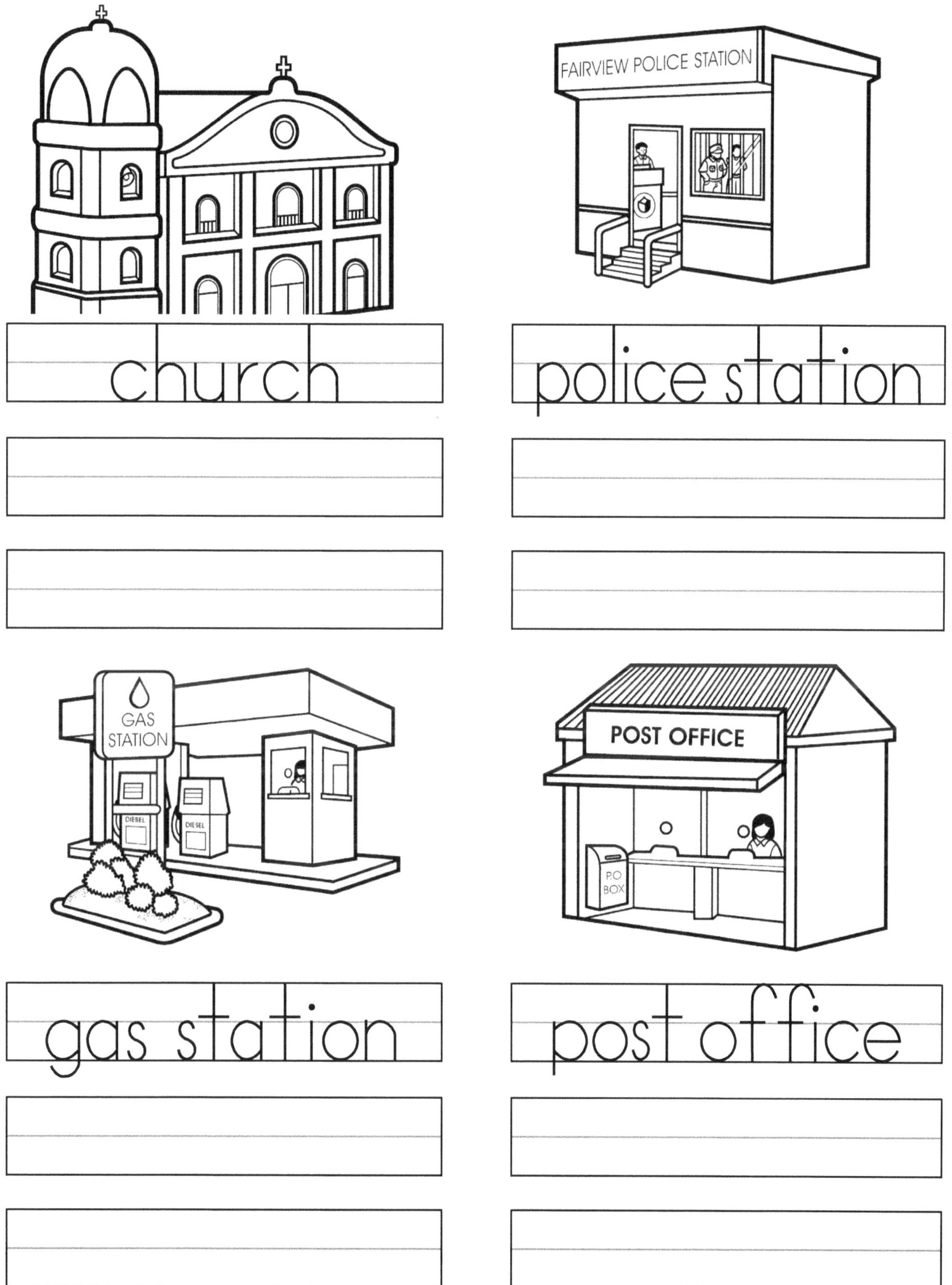
FAIRVIEW POLICE STATION
church
police station
GAS
STATION
DIESEL
DIESEL
POST OFFICE
P.O
BOX
gas station
post office

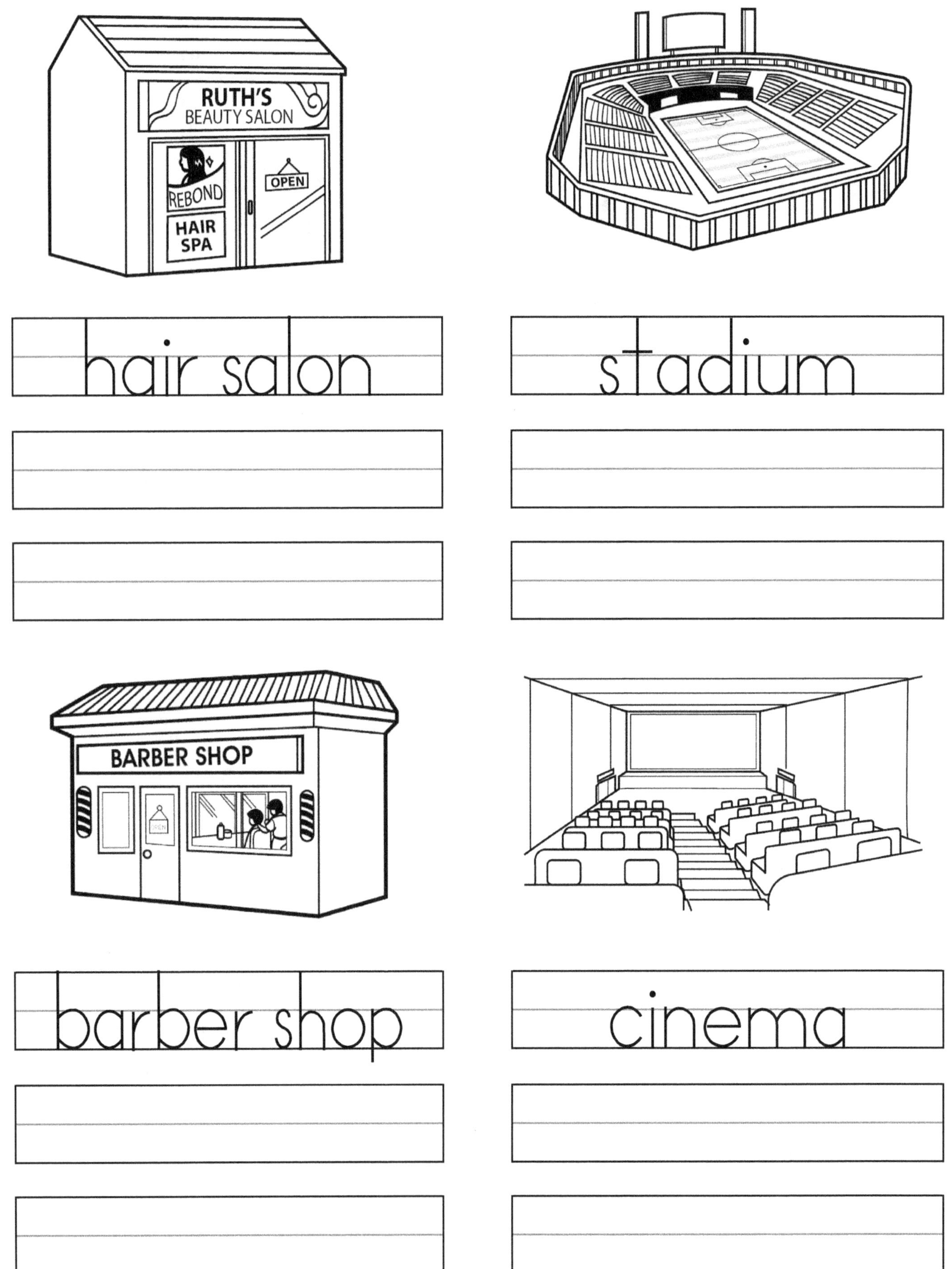
RUTH'S
BEAUTY SALON
REBOND
HAIR SPA
OPEN
hair salon
stadium
BARBER SHOP
barber shop
cinema

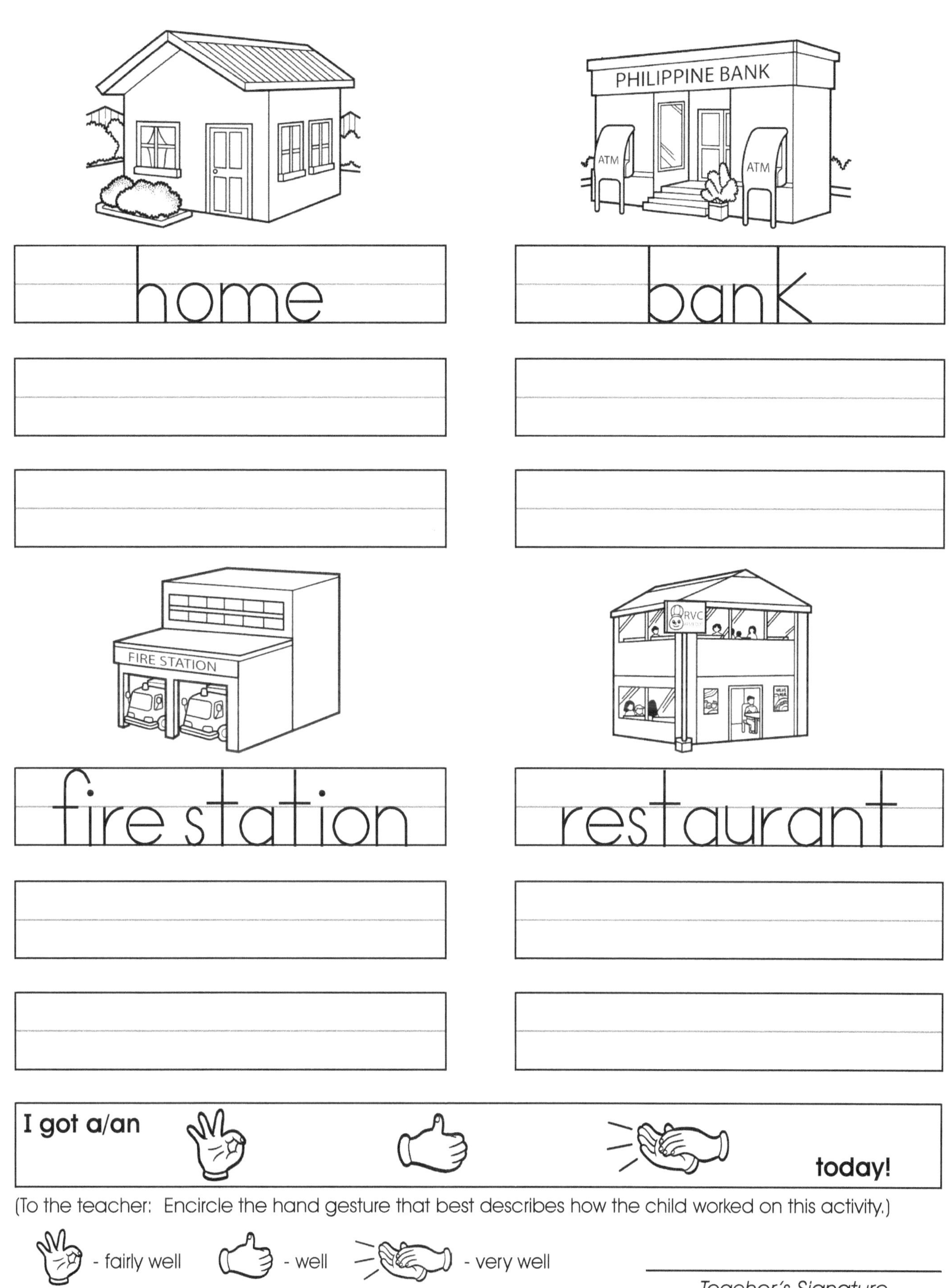
PHILIPPINE BANK
ATM
ATM
home
bank
FIRE STATION
RVC
fire station
restaurant
I got a/an
today!
(To the teacher: Encircle the hand gesture that best describes how the child worked on this activity.)
- fairly well
- well
- very well
Teacher's Signature

LESSON 7 COMMUNITY HELPERS

ACTIVITY 7

Copy the names of our community helpers on the lines below each picture.

dentist	engineer	priest
barber	mason	postman

pilot
driver
vendor
Aa
teacher
farmer
fireman

(To the teacher: Encircle the hand gesture that best describes how the child worked on this activity.)

- fairly well - well - very well

Teacher's Signature

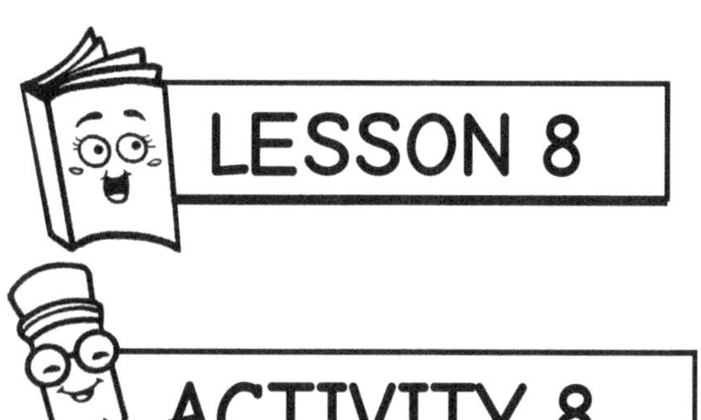

COPYING NAMES OF PLACES

Copy the names of places on the lines. Leave equal spaces between words.

Polangui, Albay

Lipa, Batangas

Imus, Cavite

Metro Davao

Araneta Coliseum

Banaue Rice Terraces

First RVC Building

Hundred Islands

Mayon Volcano

Western Samar

Xavierville Avenue

Puerto Princesa, Palawan

Quezon City

Tayabas, Quezon

Vigan, Ilocos Sur

Urdaneta, Pangasinan

31 Iceland Street

Naga City

Iba, Zambales

Chocolate Hills

Juban, Sorsogon

Gapan, Nueva Ecija

Kalinga-Apayao

The Steppingstone School

Hagonoy, Bulacan

I got a/an **today!**

(To the teacher: Encircle the hand gesture that best describes how the child worked on this activity.)

- fairly well - well - very well

Teacher's Signature

COPYING NAMES OF PEOPLE

ACTIVITY 9

Copy the names of people on the lines. Leave enough space between names.

Jackie Lee

Jocelyn D. Mercado

Bradley Dela Torre

Richard Bernardino

Ronnie C. Fedelino

Zhayne Villaflor

Jennifer T. Umali

Geneva A. Hagedorn

Miguel dela Cruz, Jr.

Sofia Robes

Kris Erwin N. Irving

Bonna Quizon

I got a/an **today!**

(To the teacher: Encircle the hand gesture that best describes how the child worked on this activity.)

- fairly well - well - very well

Teacher's Signature

ACTIVITY 10

Write your full name five times.

I got a/an **today!**

(To the teacher: Encircle the hand gesture that best describes how the child worked on this activity.)

- fairly well - well - very well

Teacher's Signature

COPYING PHRASES

Copy the phrases on the lines. Leave enough space between words.

a purple dress

five pretty girls

two cups of coffee

a big, red balloon

two white horses

an elegant gown

full of surprises

a simple house

an expensive gift

seven young boys

pink roses

eight brave men

I got a/an **today!**

(To the teacher: Encircle the hand gesture that best describes how the child worked on this activity.)

- fairly well - well - very well

Teacher's Signature

Copy the long phrases on the lines. Leave enough space between words.

a glass of cold, fresh juice

a plate of seedless grapes

six men in the forest

three bags on the table

painting the room with blue

rainbow in the sky

my favorite chocolate cake

delicious food on the table

ten pairs of colorful slippers

dogs sleeping under the tree

sweet candies in the jar

nine ducks in the farm

a big monkey-eating eagle

I got a/an **today!**

(To the teacher: Encircle the hand gesture that best describes how the child worked on this activity.)

- fairly well - well - very well

Teacher's Signature

COPYING TITLES

Copy the titles on the lines. Leave enough space between words.

Someone Like You

Three Little Ducklings

Dhara's Favorite Dress

The Big, Black Sheep

The King's Inn

I got a/an **today!**

(To the teacher: Encircle the hand gesture that best describes how the child worked on this activity.)

 - fairly well  - well  - very well

Teacher's Signature

LESSON 12 COPYING SENTENCES

ACTIVITY 14

Copy the sentences on the lines. Leave enough space between words.

James is a good painter.

I want to be a doctor someday.

Anabel wakes up early in the morning.

She looks elegant in her gown.

My mother loves to cook pasta.

I like to eat spaghetti and fried chicken.

Kurt is a very handsome boy.

The farmer rested under the tree.

Bea is a well-loved actress.

We went to the zoo last Sunday.

My brother bought apples and peaches.

Our teachers are having a meeting.

My father works in the office.

Tony gave Ben a big house.

There are many colorful flowers in the garden.

The old man lives alone in the farm.

Children love to play outdoor games.

We will go to the beach next week.

Aira is a beautiful girl.

I got a/an **today!**

(To the teacher: Encircle the hand gesture that best describes how the child worked on this activity.)

- fairly well - well - very well

____

Teacher's Signature

LESSON 13 COPYING PARAGRAPHS

ACTIVITY 15

Copy the paragraphs on the space provided below each one. Observe correct spacing between words.

My Dog and My Cat

I have a dog and a cat.

My dog's name is Bantay.

My cat's name is Kitkat.

Wowie's Cookies

Wowie loves to bake.

She bakes tasty cookies.

I like to eat her cookies.

I got a/an **today!**

(To the teacher: Encircle the hand gesture that best describes how the child worked on this activity.)

- fairly well - well - very well

Teacher's Signature

LESSON 14 COPYING HOMEWORK

ACTIVITY 16

Copy the following on the space provided below. Observe correct spacing between words.

Jan.	Homework
10,	1. Cut out pictures of animals.
2019	2. Paste them onto an oslo paper.
	Parent's Signature

I got a/an    **today!**

(To the teacher: Encircle the hand gesture that best describes how the child worked on this activity.)

 - fairly well  - well  - very well

____
Teacher's Signature

PROGRESS CHART
THIRD QUARTER

NAME: ______________________________ LEVEL: ____________

Activity	What I Got			Quiz	No. of Items	My Score
	fairly well	well	very well			
1						
2						
3						
4						
5						
6						
7						
8						
9						
10						
11						
12						
13						
14						
15						
16						
TOTAL				TOTAL		

______________________________ ______________________________

Parent's/Guardian's Signature Teacher's Signature

Legend: fairly well well very well

FOURTH QUARTER

Teacher's Objectives and Student Evaluation

Lesson	*At the end of the activities, the child should be able to:*			
1	1. master basic writing movements necessary in writing cursive			
	2. use directionality in forming slants, curves, round and sharp tops, loops, and ovals			
2	3. write the lowercase letters of the alphabet in cursive			
3	4. write the uppercase letters of the alphabet in cursive, starting with the vowels			
4	5. write the uppercase letters of the alphabet in cursive, emphasizing the consonants			
5	6. begin writing in cursive, starting with joining two letters together			
6	7. write his or her name in cursive			
7	8. copy different words in cursive			
8	9. copy short and long phrases in cursive, giving emphasis on proper spacing between words			
9	10. copy sentences in cursive, with emphasis on proper spacing between words			

Legend:  fairly well  well  very well

PREPARING TO WRITE IN CURSIVE

BASIC WRITING MOVEMENTS

Tall and Short Slants

Trace the broken lines. Follow the direction of the arrows.

Make your own tall and short slants. Observe proper spacing.

I got a/an ... **today!**

(To the teacher: Encircle the hand gesture that best describes how the child worked on this activity.)

- fairly well
- well
- very well

Teacher's Signature

Tall and Short Under-Curves

ACTIVITY 2

Trace the broken lines. Follow the direction of the arrows. Start from top to bottom on the first two rows. Start from bottom to top on the third row.

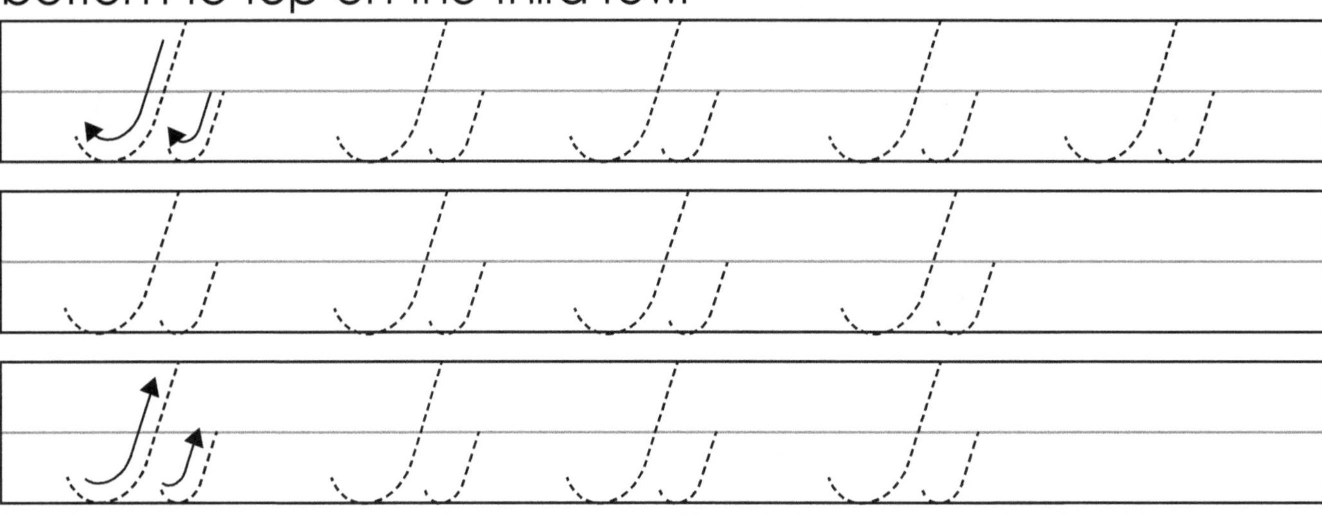

Make your own under-curves. Start from top to bottom on the first two rows and from bottom to top on the third row. Observe proper spacing.

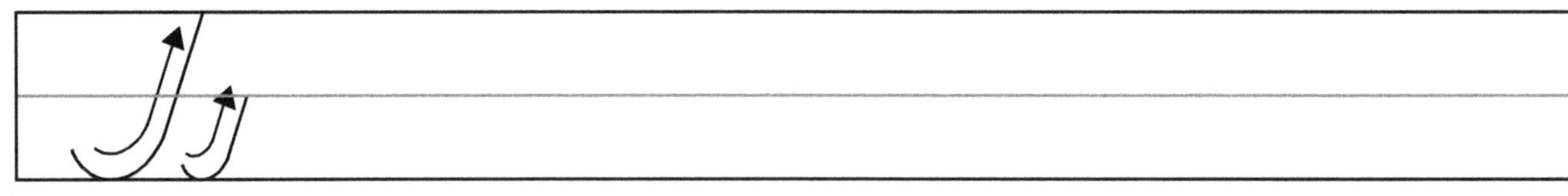

I got a/an    **today!**

(To the teacher: Encircle the hand gesture that best describes how the child worked on this activity.)

 - fairly well  - well - very well

____
Teacher's Signature

Tall and Short Over-Curves

ACTIVITY 3

Trace the broken lines. Follow the direction of the arrows. Start from top to bottom on the first two rows. Start from bottom to top on the third row.

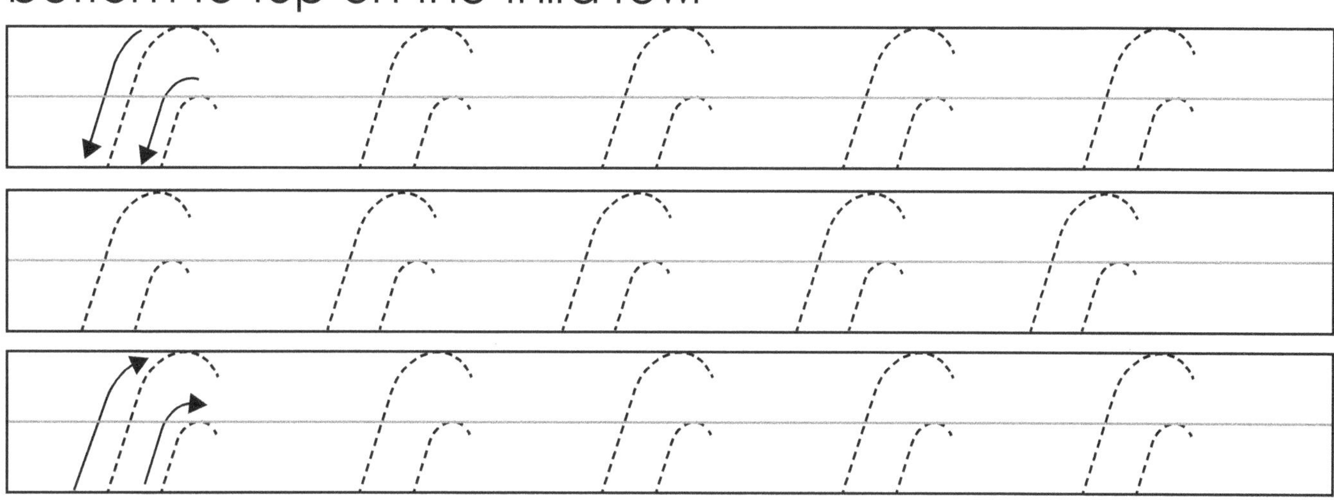

Make your own over-curves. Start from top to bottom on the first two rows and from bottom to top on the third row. Observe proper spacing.

I got a/an    **today!**

(To the teacher: Encircle the hand gesture that best describes how the child worked on this activity.)

 - fairly well  - well  - very well

____
Teacher's Signature

ACTIVITY 4

Double Curves

Trace the broken lines. Follow the direction of the arrow.

Make your own double curves. Observe proper spacing.

I got a/an ... today!

(To the teacher: Encircle the hand gesture that best describes how the child worked on this activity.)

- fairly well

- well

- very well

____

Teacher's Signature

Over- and Under-Curves

ACTIVITY 5

Trace the broken lines. Follow the direction of the arrows. Start from top to bottom on the first two rows. Start from bottom to top on the third row.

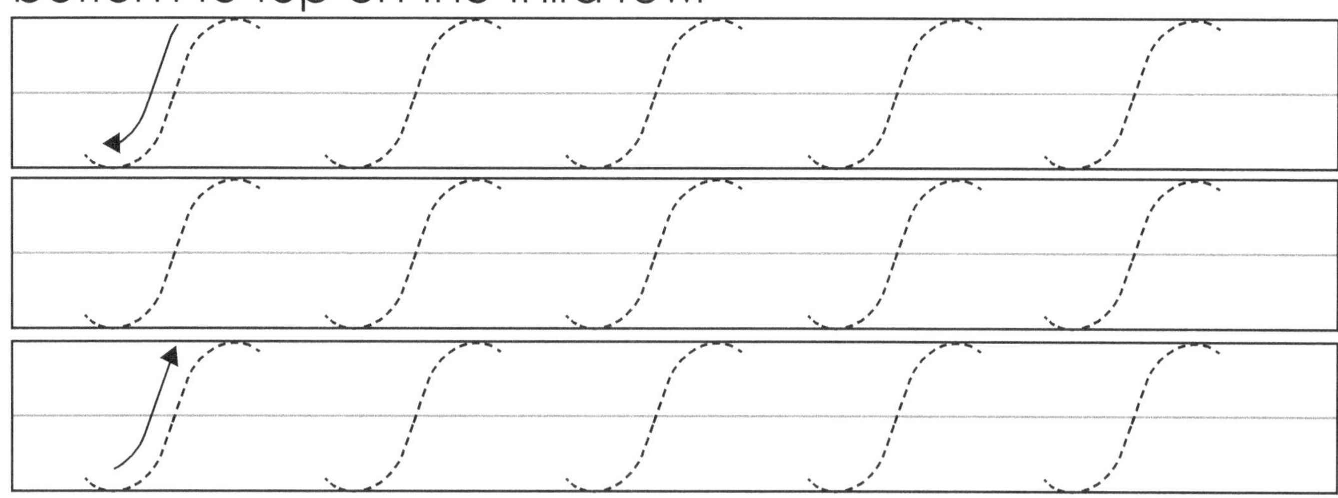

Make your own over- and under-curves. Start from top to bottom on the first two rows and from bottom to top on the third row. Observe proper spacing.

I got a/an **today!**

(To the teacher: Encircle the hand gesture that best describes how the child worked on this activity.)

 - fairly well  - well - very well

Teacher's Signature

Round Tops

Trace the broken lines. Follow the direction of the arrow.

Make your own round tops. Observe proper spacing.

I got a/an    **today!**

(To the teacher: Encircle the hand gesture that best describes how the child worked on this activity.)

 - fairly well  - well  - very well

____

Teacher's Signature

ACTIVITY 7

Sharp Tops

Trace the broken lines. Follow the direction of the arrows.

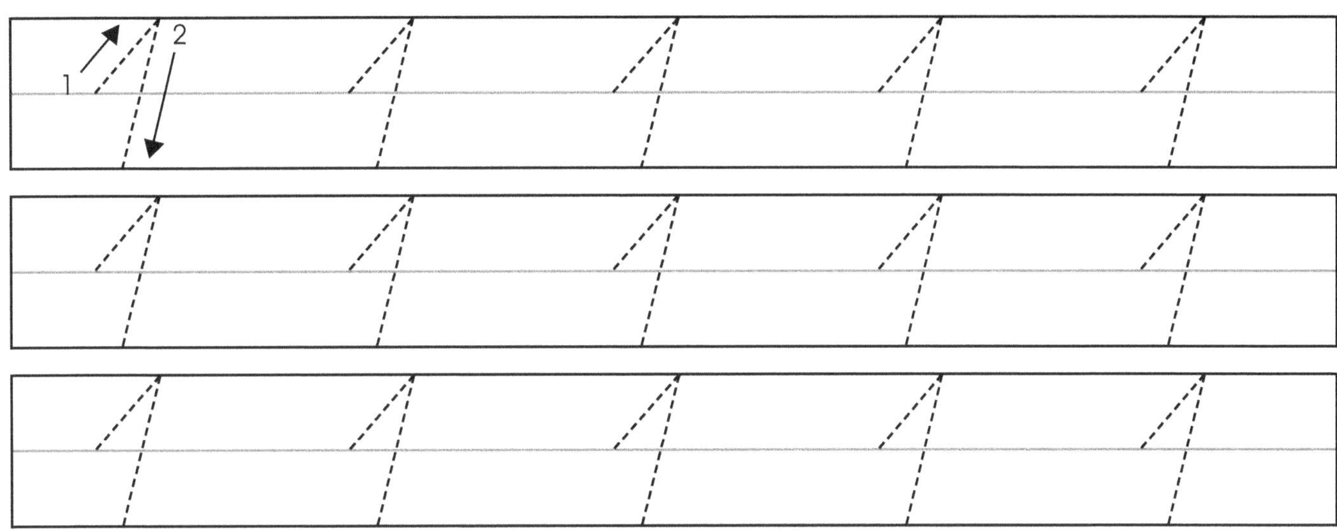

Make your own sharp tops. Observe proper spacing.

I got a/an    **today!**

(To the teacher: Encircle the hand gesture that best describes how the child worked on this activity.)

 - fairly well  - well  - very well

____
Teacher's Signature

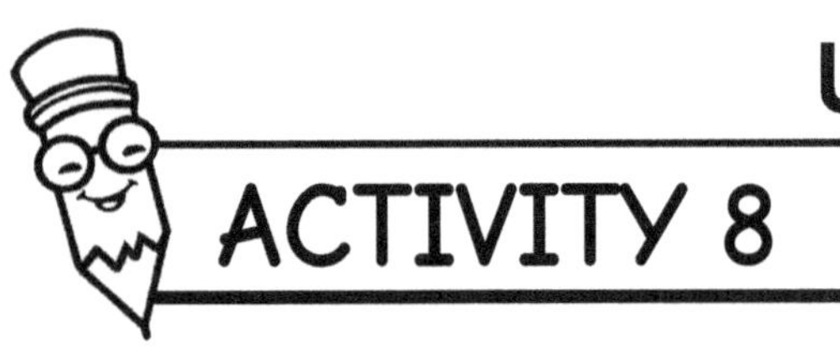

Upward Loops

ACTIVITY 8

Trace the broken lines. Follow the direction of the arrows.

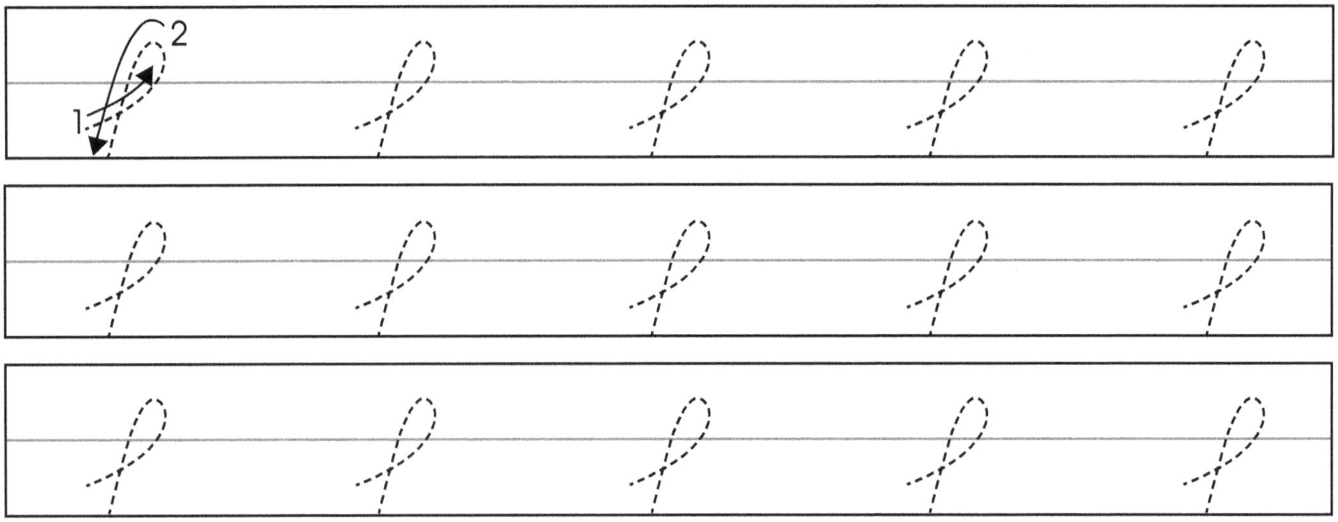

Make your own upward loops. Observe proper spacing.

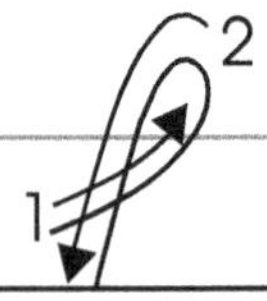

I got a/an 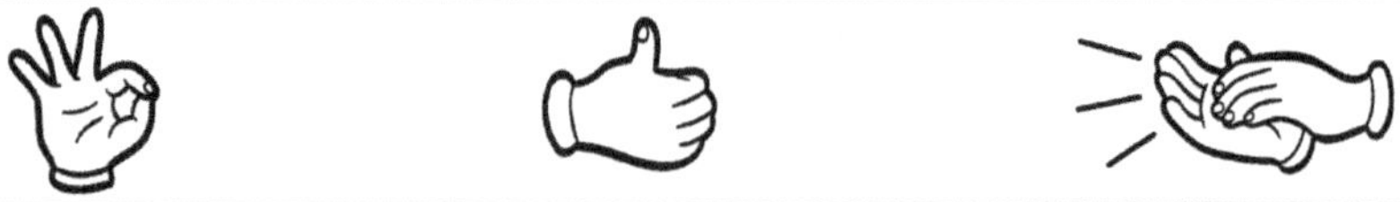 **today!**

(To the teacher: Encircle the hand gesture that best describes how the child worked on this activity.)

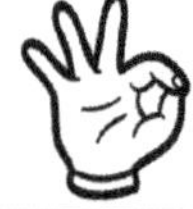

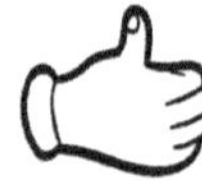

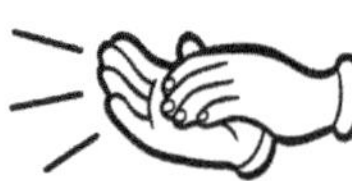

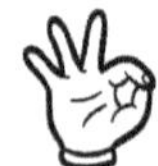

 - fairly well - well - very well

____

Teacher's Signature

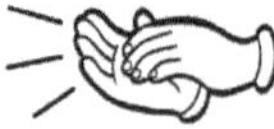

Downward Loops

ACTIVITY 9

Trace the broken lines. Follow the direction of the arrows.

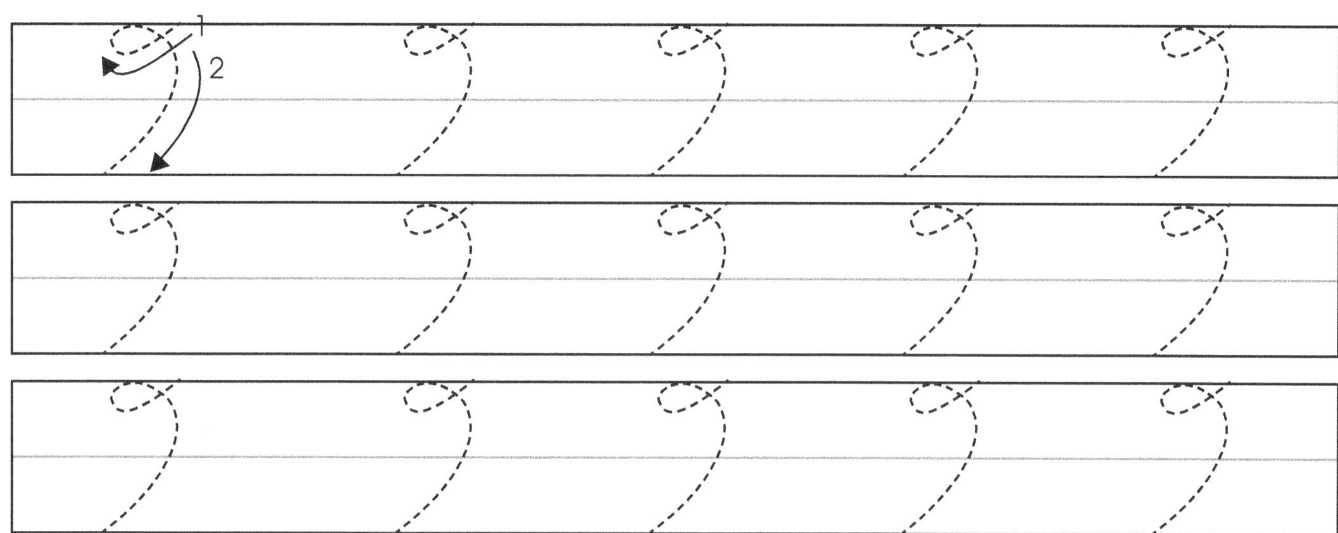

Make your own downward loops. Observe proper spacing.

I got a/an    **today!**

(To the teacher: Encircle the hand gesture that best describes how the child worked on this activity.)

 - fairly well  - well  - very well

____
Teacher's Signature

Push and Pulls

ACTIVITY 10

Trace the broken lines. Follow the direction of the arrows.

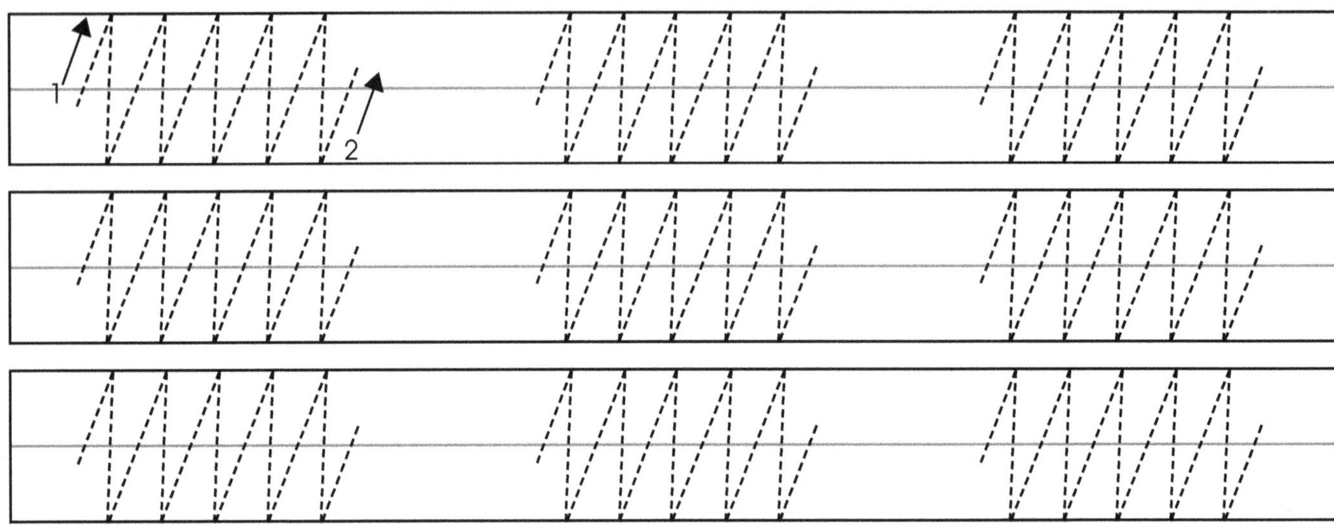

Make your own push and pulls. Observe proper spacing.

I got a/an    **today!**

(To the teacher: Encircle the hand gesture that best describes how the child worked on this activity.)

 - fairly well  - well  - very well

Teacher's Signature

ACTIVITY 11

Direct Ovals

Make your own direct ovals. Follow the direction of the arrows. Observe proper spacing.

1 2 1 2 1 2

Indirect Ovals

Make your own indirect ovals. Follow the direction of the arrows.Observe proper spacing.

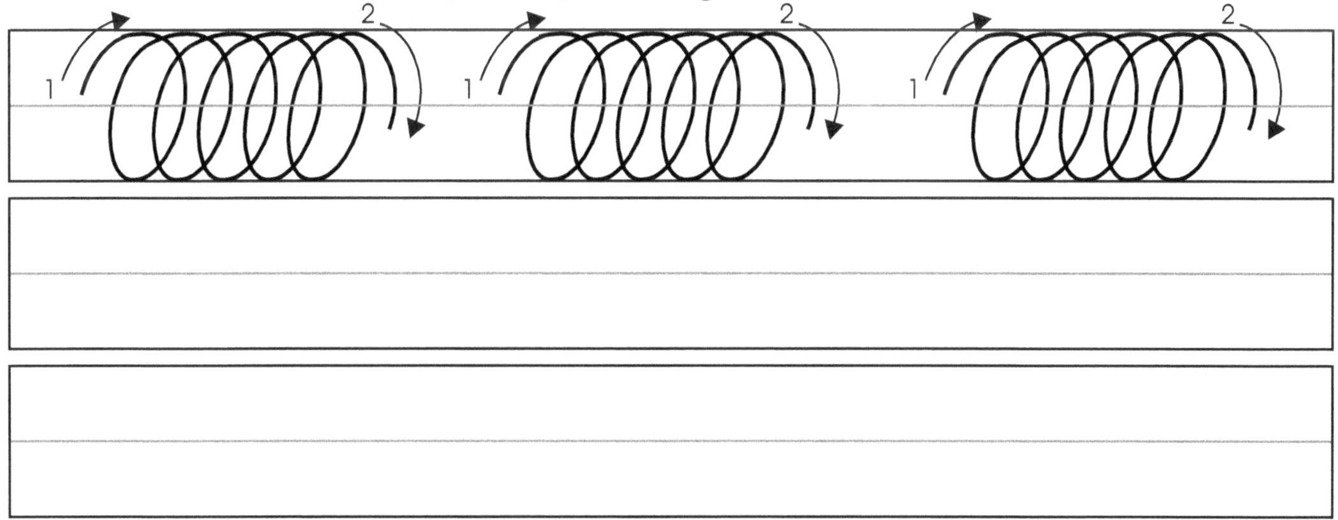

I got a/an    **today!**

(To the teacher: Encircle the hand gesture that best describes how the child worked on this activity.)

 - fairly well  - well 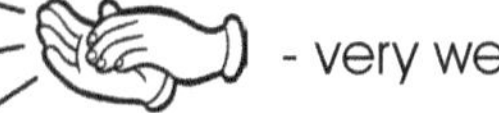 - very well

____

Teacher's Signature

LESSON 2 THE LOWERCASE LETTERS OF THE ALPHABET

THE VOWELS

ACTIVITY 12

Trace the vowel letters. Follow the direction of the arrows.

a	e	i	o	u
a	e	i	o	u
a	e	i	o	u
a	e	i	o	u
a	e	i	o	u
a	e	i	o	u

I got a/an    **today!**

(To the teacher: Encircle the hand gesture that best describes how the child worked on this activity.)

 - fairly well  - well  - very well

____
Teacher's Signature

Make your own letters using the correct strokes. Write each letter five times in each row, observing proper spacing between letters.

a

e

i

o

u

I got a/an    **today!**

(To the teacher: Encircle the hand gesture that best describes how the child worked on this activity.)

 - fairly well  - well  - very well

____
Teacher's Signature

THE CONSONANTS

Short Letters

Trace the letters. Follow the direction of the arrows.

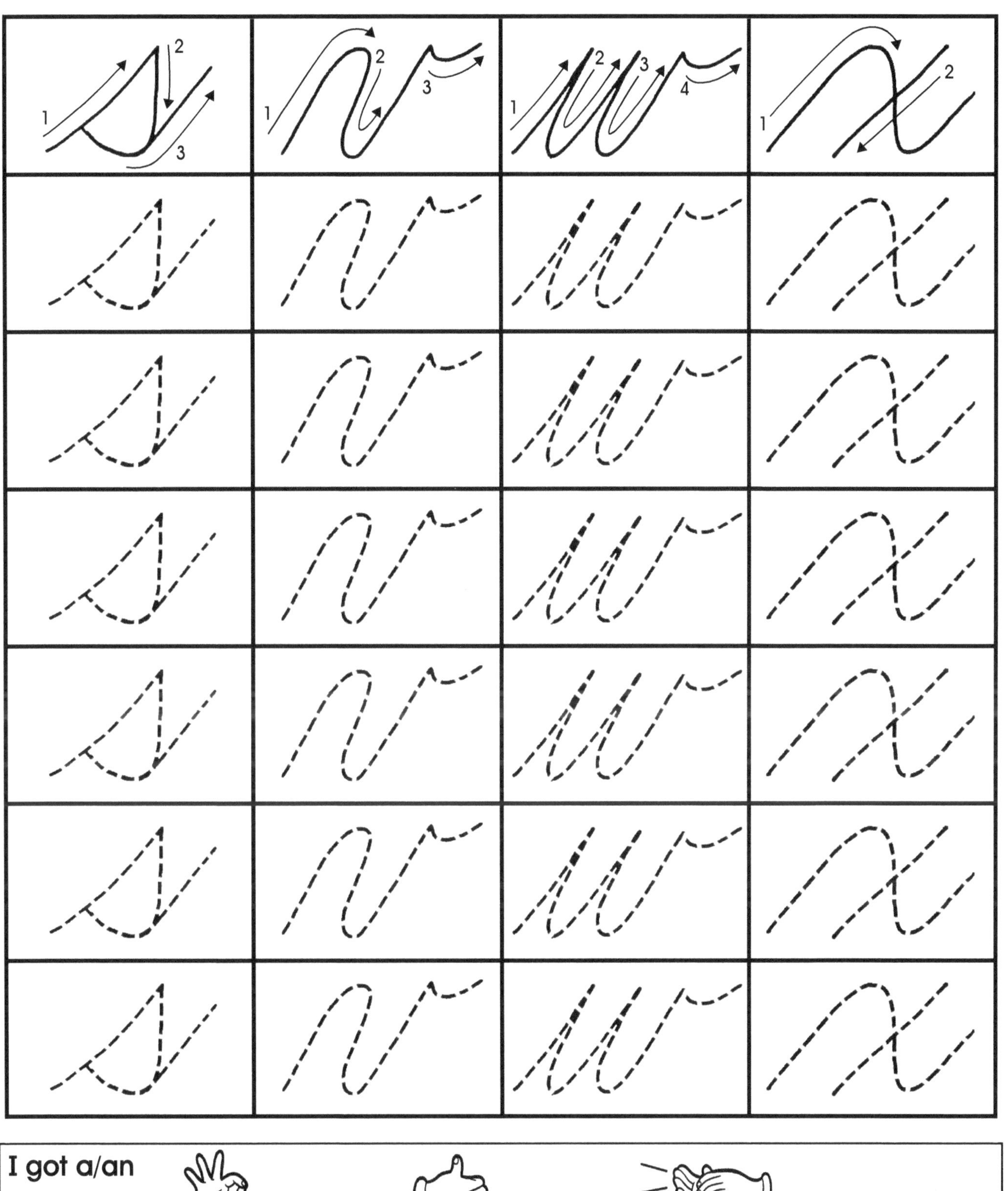

I got a/an [fairly well] [well] [very well] today!

(To the teacher: Encircle the hand gesture that best describes how the child worked on this activity.)

[fairly well hand gesture] - fairly well [well hand gesture] - well [very well hand gesture] - very well

____
Teacher's Signature

ACTIVITY 15

Make your own letters using the correct strokes. Write each letter five times in each row, observing proper spacing between letters.

c

m

n

r

s

v

w

x

I got a/an **today!**

(To the teacher: Encircle the hand gesture that best describes how the child worked on this activity.)

 - fairly well  - well  - very well

____

Teacher's Signature

Tall Letters

ACTIVITY 16

Trace the letters. Follow the direction of the arrows.

b	d	h	k	l	t
b	d	h	k	l	t
b	d	h	k	l	t
b	d	h	k	l	t
b	d	h	k	l	t
b	d	h	k	l	t
b	d	h	k	l	t

I got a/an    **today!**

(To the teacher: Encircle the hand gesture that best describes how the child worked on this activity.)

 - fairly well  - well 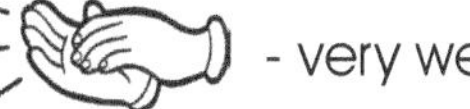 - very well

____
Teacher's Signature

Make your own letters using the correct strokes. Write each letter five times in each row, observing proper spacing between letters.

b

d

h

k

l

t

I got a/an today!

(To the teacher: Encircle the hand gesture that best describes how the child worked on this activity.)

- fairly well - well - very well

Teacher's Signature

Tail Letters

ACTIVITY 18

Trace the letters. Follow the direction of the arrows.

f	g	j	p	q	y	z
f	g	j	p	q	y	z
f	g	j	p	q	y	z
f	g	j	p	q	y	z
f	g	j	p	q	y	z
f	g	j	p	q	y	z
f	g	j	p	q	y	z
f	g	j	p	q	y	z

I got a/an today!

(To the teacher: Encircle the hand gesture that best describes how the child worked on this activity.)

 - fairly well  - well  - very well

____
Teacher's Signature

ACTIVITY 19

Make your own letters using the correct strokes. Write each letter five times in each row obeserving proper spacing between letters.

f

g

j

p

q

y

z

I got a/an **today!**

(To the teacher: Encircle the hand gesture that best describes how the child worked on this activity.)

- fairly well  - well  - very well

Teacher's Signature

Copy the lowercase letters of the alphabet.

a b c d e f g

h i j k l m n

o p q r s t u

v w x y z

I got a/an    today!

(To the teacher: Encircle the hand gesture that best describes how the child worked on this activity.)

 - fairly well  - well  - very well

____
Teacher's Signature

THE UPPERCASE LETTERS OF THE ALPHABET

THE VOWELS

ACTIVITY 21

Trace the vowel letters. Follow the direction of the arrows.

A	E	I	O	U
A	E	I	O	U
A	E	I	O	U
A	E	I	O	U
A	E	I	O	U
A	E	I	O	U

I got a/an    **today!**

(To the teacher: Encircle the hand gesture that best describes how the child worked on this activity.)

 - fairly well  - well  - very well

____
Teacher's Signature

Make your own letters using the correct strokes. Write each letter five times in each row, observing proper spacing between letters.

A

E

I

O

U

I got a/an **today!**

(To the teacher: Encircle the hand gesture that best describes how the child worked on this activity.)

- fairly well - well - very well

Teacher's Signature

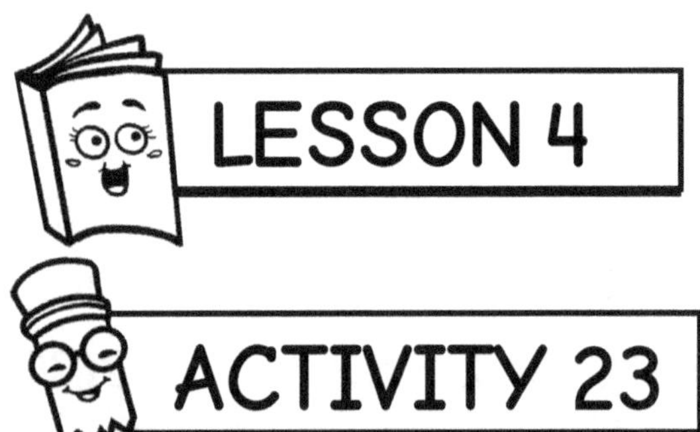

THE CONSONANTS

Trace the consonant letters. Follow the direction of the arrows.

B	C	D	F	G	H	J
B	C	D	F	G	H	J
B	C	D	F	G	H	J
B	C	D	F	G	H	J
B	C	D	F	G	H	J

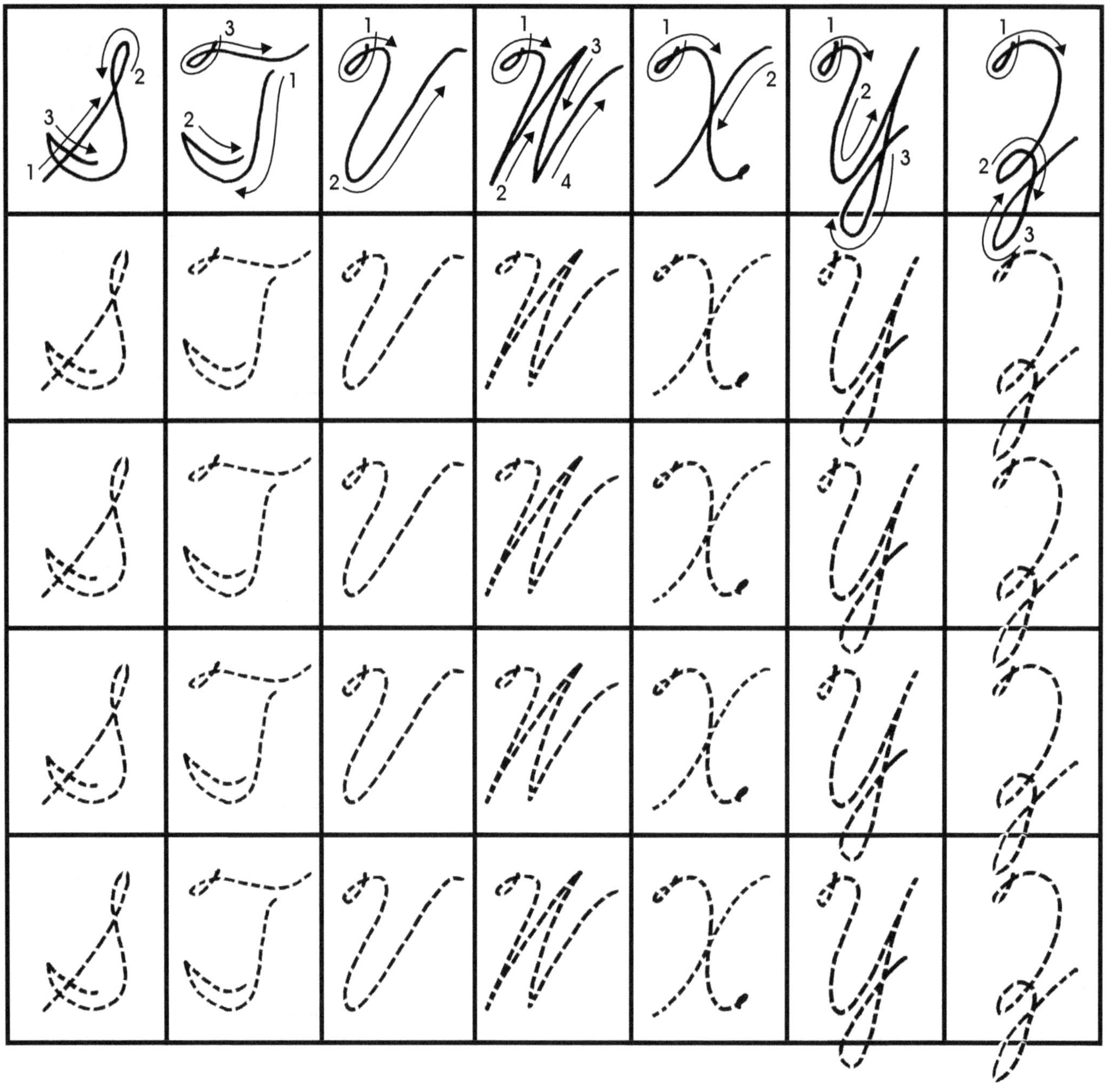

I got a/an    today!

(To the teacher: Encircle the hand gesture that best describes how the child worked on this activity.)

 - fairly well  - well  - very well

Teacher's Signature

ACTIVITY 24

Write the letters below using the correct strokes. Write each letter five times in each row, observing proper spacing between letters.

B

C

D

F

G

H

I

K

L

M

N

P

Q

R

(To the teacher: Encircle the hand gesture that best describes how the child worked on this activity.)

- fairly well - well - very well

Teacher's Signature

ACTIVITY 25

Copy the uppercase letters of the alphabet.

A B C D E F G

H I J K L M N

O P Q R S T U

V W X Y Z

I got a/an    **today!**

(To the teacher: Encircle the hand gesture that best describes how the child worked on this activity.)

 - fairly well  - well  - very well

____

Teacher's Signature

LESSON 5 JOINING LETTERS

ACTIVITY 26

Trace and copy the two letter combinations. Observe proper spacing between each letter pair.

ie ie ie ie ie

ie

ie

iv iv iv iv iv

iv

iv

I got a/an today!

(To the teacher: Encircle the hand gesture that best describes how the child worked on this activity.)

 - fairly well  - well  - very well

Teacher's Signature

ACTIVITY 27

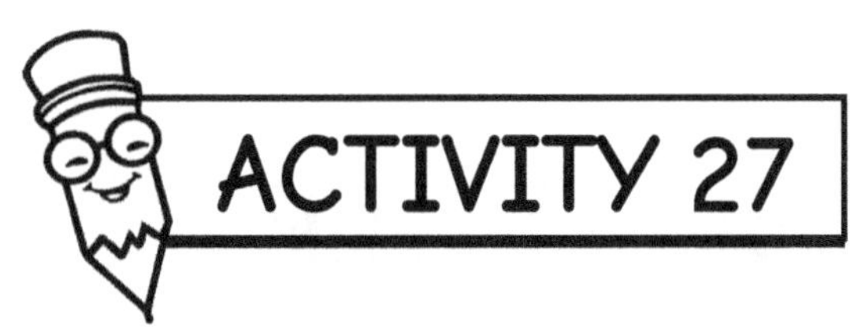

Trace and copy the two letter combinations. Observe proper spacing between each letter pair.

ta ta ta ta ta

ta

ta

do do do do do

do

do

I got a/an   **today!**

(To the teacher: Encircle the hand gesture that best describes how the child worked on this activity.)

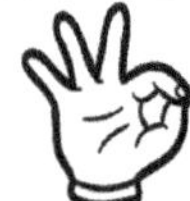

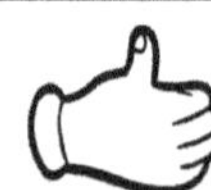

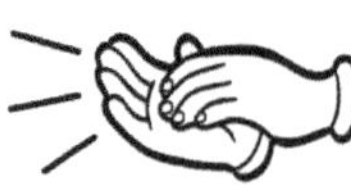

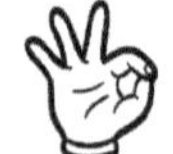

 - fairly well - well - very well

____
Teacher's Signature

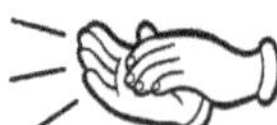

ACTIVITY 28

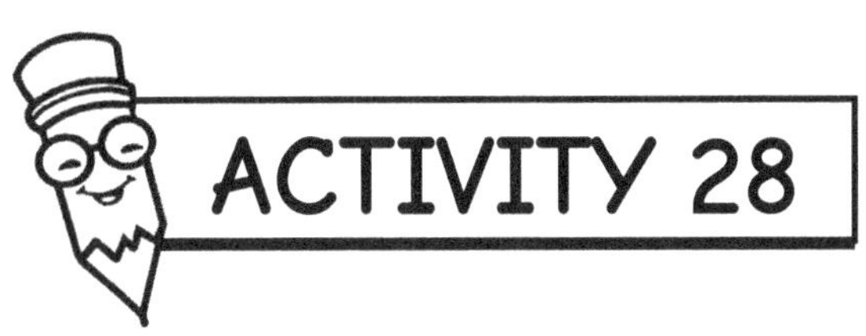

Trace and copy the two letter combinations. Observe proper spacing between each letter pair.

ba ba ba ba ba

ba

ba

ke ke ke ke ke

ke

ke

I got a/an   **today!**

(To the teacher: Encircle the hand gesture that best describes how the child worked on this activity.)

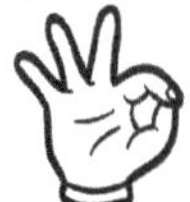

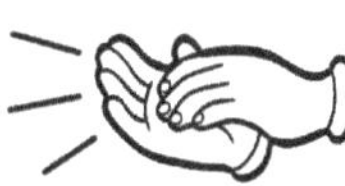

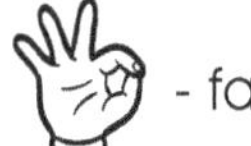

 - fairly well - well - very well

____

Teacher's Signature

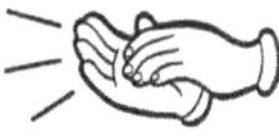

ACTIVITY 29

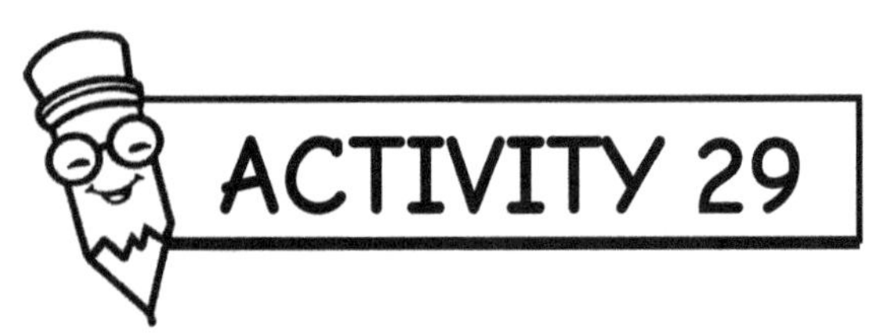

Trace and copy the two letter combinations. Observe proper spacing between each letter pair.

up up up up up

up

up

ig ig ig ig ig

ig

ig

I got a/an 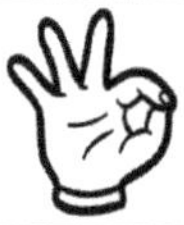 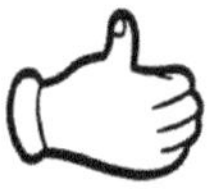 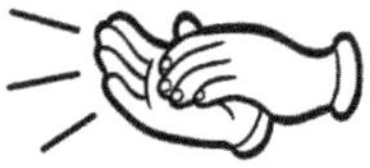 **today!**

(To the teacher: Encircle the hand gesture that best describes how the child worked on this activity.)

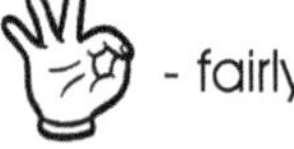

 - fairly well 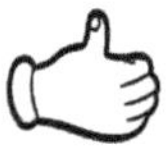 - well - very well

____
Teacher's Signature

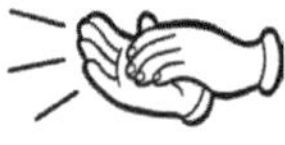

ACTIVITY 30

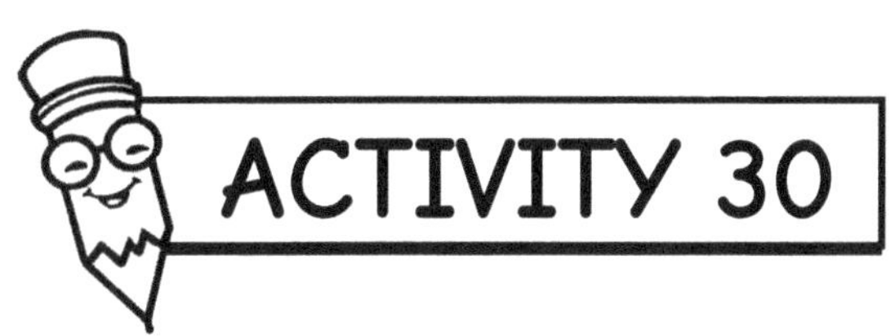

Trace and copy the two letter combinations. Observe proper spacing between each letter pair.

gh gh gh gh gh

gh

gh

fl fl fl fl fl

fl

fl

I got a/an 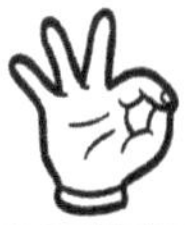 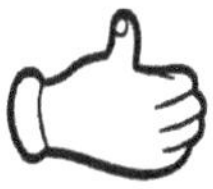 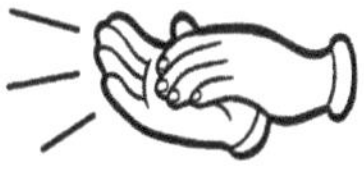 today!

(To the teacher: Encircle the hand gesture that best describes how the child worked on this activity.)

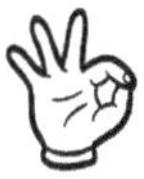 - fairly well 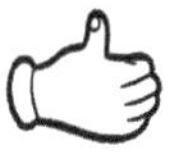 - well 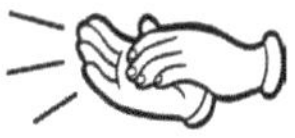 - very well

____
Teacher's Signature

WRITING NAME IN CURSIVE

Practice writing your name in cursive form. Write it three times below.

My name is

My name is

My name is

I got a/an today!

(To the teacher: Encircle the hand gesture that best describes how the child worked on this activity.)

 - fairly well  - well 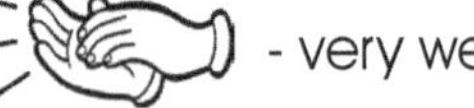 - very well

Teacher's Signature

LESSON 7 COPYING WORDS

ACTIVITY 32

Copy the words on the lines below.

arm	wine	vase

cone	sum	wax

dear belt lord

kind host kettle

envy pray juggle

yolk gift quail

bible quarit locks

vest stand zigzag

I got a/an today!

(To the teacher: Encircle the hand gesture that best describes how the child worked on this activity.)

- fairly well - well - very well

Teacher's Signature

LESSON 8 COPYING PHRASES

ACTIVITY 33

Copy the phrases on the lines below.

a huge jug	*tiny stone*
orange wall	*painted box*

a quiet zoo

five vans

black cat

an old man

I got a/an ... today!

(To the teacher: Encircle the hand gesture that best describes how the child worked on this activity.)

- fairly well - well - very well

Teacher's Signature

LESSON 9 COPYING SENTENCES

ACTIVITY 34

Copy the sentences on the lines below.

My teacher is pretty.

Grandfather has a jack.

I saw a big van.

The queen sits on a rock.

Her friend went to the zoo.

Peter has a new vest.

I got a/an (fairly well) (well) (very well) today!

(To the teacher: Encircle the hand gesture that best describes how the child worked on this activity.)

- fairly well - well - very well

____
Teacher's Signature

PROGRESS CHART
FOURTH QUARTER

NAME: ______________________________ LEVEL: ____________

Activity	What I Got			Quiz	No. of Items	My Score
1						
2						
3						
4						
5						
6						
7						
8						
9						
10						
11						
12						
13						
14						
15						
16						
17						
18						
19						
20						
21						
22						
23						
24						
25						
26						
27						
28						
29						
30						
31						
32						
33						
34						
TOTAL				TOTAL		

______________________________ ______________________________

Parent's/Guardian's Signature Teacher's Signature

Legend: fairly well  well very well

HAZEL DOMINGO BABIANO

Hazel Domingo Babiano is the directress of the Steppingstone Progressivist School, which has campuses in Fairview, Quezon City and Caloocan City.

She leads a dynamic life in the education field as an Instructional Manager for the Department of Education in the National Capital Region, an Educational Consultant for the Child Development Center of Sirkulo ng Kababaihan sa Pasig (SIKAPIN), Vice-Chairperson on Education, Urban Poor Institute for Community Building (UPICOB), and official trainor/facilitator of BKP (Bagong Kulturang Pinoy) Philippines.

She finished both her degrees in Bachelor of Arts in Psychology and her Masters in Education, major in Special Education from the University of the Philippines.

ACKNOWLEDGMENT

This book wouldn't have been possible without the precious assistance and support of the following people:

- my awesome kids, the sources of my inspiration — Donovan, Alathea, Bohari, and Adzel — for the overwhelming support, understanding, concern, love, and yes, for everything;
- Dada and Aeden — for adding color to my life;
- the teachers and staff of STEPPINGSTONE — Layra L. del Rosario, Mitchel T. Pula, Eva Mascariola, Lizette Don, and Ofelieta O. Saladaga — for taking charge of the school while I am busy writing books and conducting seminars;
- Jean L. Pascual — for helping me with the other details of this book;
- Susan S. Nuñes — for guiding me through my spiritual growth;
- my sisters, Josie, Loida, and Lorna — for being with me through rain and shine;
- my publishers — the fabulous Raymund and the alluring Isabel Catabijan — for the special bonding spiced with some "jokes";
- the magnificent sisters, Regine and Wowie — for guiding me through the digital aspects of book-writing;
- the staff of St. Matthew's Publishing — Sarah, Maricar, Janet, Josie, Gina, Darren, Orly, Gio, Eunice, Sol and, of course, Rollie — for all the fun and for their patience with my "kakulitan";
- the gorgeous agents, sub-agents and artists of Saint Matthew's Publishing — for their hard work and perseverance;
- all teachers — not only for helping me touch the lives of children, but also for making a difference in all the lives that we touch;
- all children — for inspiring me and helping me learn the greatest lessons in life;
- my great love — for believing in me and bringing back my self-esteem, for the laughter, the words of encouragement, the many sacrifices, the respect, the love, and the simple gestures of kindness... for being my best friend... and for trudging with me through life's endless journey;
- above all, our Almighty God — for the good health and for the gifts of humor, wisdom, perseverance, resiliency, and extraordinary strength; and for the outpouring blessings despite the tough journey... thanks, Lord!

Hazel Domingo Babiano